IN PLACE

In Place

Stories of Landscape and Identity
from the American West

Barbara Allen Bogart

Barbara Allen Bogart

High Plains Press

Cover and interior illustrations
by Mary Patricia Ettinger

Illustrations © 1995 Mary Patricia Ettinger

Library of Congress Cataloging-in-Publication Data

Bogart, Barbara Allen
In place: stories of landscape and identity from the American West
Barbara Allen Bogart
p. cm.
Includes bibliographical references.
ISBN 0-931271-27-4 (soft: acid free)
1. West (U.S.)--Social life and customs.
2. Landscape--West (U.S.)
3. Oral tradition--West (U.S.)
4. Group identity--West (U.S.)
I. Title.
F596.B65   1994   94-34241
978--dc20   CIP

HIGH PLAINS PRESS
539 CASSA ROAD
GLENDO, WYOMING 82213

for my mother and father
who saw to it that I was born a westerner
and for Dan
with whom I have found a home in the West

⪼ Contents ⪻

Introduction
❧ Finding Ourselves in Place ❧

"**H**OW DO WE KNOW WHO WE ARE**," asks writer Wendell Berry, "until we first know where we are?" We answer both questions, I believe, when we tell stories about the places in which we live. That is what the stories in this book are about: the links between place and identity.

The book has grown out of a long-standing and deep-seated interest in story that had its origins in my first field experience as a folklorist. As a neophyte graduate student, I set off in the summer of 1974, armed with a tape recorder and a rudimentary understanding of folklore, to meet and interview a 74-year-old man who lived in a tiny community in northern California. When I met him, Sid Morrison was living in the house that his grandfather had built. Coming as I did from a peripatetic existence in southern California, I was intrigued at meeting someone who had spent his entire life in one place and was apparently happy to be so rooted.

I had come to Sid with the idea of asking him about local folklore—songs, superstitions, games, and the like. But what he wanted to tell was what he knew and loved best: stories about people and events in his home community. Those stories were drawn from his own experiences, along with stories his father and grandfather had told and stories from neighbors and friends in the valley—all of simple, ordinary experiences, all beautifully told. What puzzled me at first was they weren't stories of the kind I had been taught to recognize as *folk*. At least I had the sense to recognize that they were stories even though they did not bear the earmarks of tradition.

Unwittingly, in the series of visits I made to record Sid's stories, I was setting a personal and professional course for myself that I am still pursuing. I had come to Sid with a passing interest in story; he fixed that interest permanently and gave it a particular twist. As I initially named this outgrowth, I was curious about how experience (history, I called it) is turned into narrative. Sid's stories were living proof of the process.

What I did not recognize at the time, what I have only recently realized, is that Sid's stories were not just about the past but also about place. A sense of place permeates his stories on a number of levels. Most obviously, perhaps, is their subject matter: all of the stories are set in and around his home valley. As he told them, he pointed out the window to indicate where each one took place. But the stories are about place on a deeper level. Sid wanted to tell them, even to a callow and ignorant stranger like me, because they expressed the essence of life in that place from his point of view. The valley he lived in and the hills surrounding it, the shore that bounded it, the river that ran through it were alive for him not just with the memories of his own experiences but with his knowledge of what had happened to others who had lived there before him. So he told his stories to all who would listen—family, friends, neighbors, and the itinerant scholar—with a passion that I see now bespoke his purpose. He was impatient with error and scornful of insincerity in people who wrote about the place from a superficial and often mistaken understanding of it. He told his stories with an emotional force that often came out in breaks in his voice and tears in his eyes. I am not sure that he felt I was to be trusted with his treasure, but he also knew that his opportunities for passing it on were limited—he had no children—so he scattered his pearls before him in a kind of desperation marked by grace. At the time I did not pay him the homage that this gentle man deserved. Perhaps that's what this book is about.

I went on to listen to other people's stories about the places they lived in, in other parts of the West. As I did so, I still believed that I was interested in how they made story out of history. Eventually, I left California for the South and then the Midwest and discovered in the process my own western identity. And that discovery generated a spark that gradually grew into a low, slow-burning fire at which I am now warming my hands and wondering. Experiencing the differences in regional cultures gave me a new angle of vision on the stories I'd recorded in the West and made me wonder if there was something about the West that made the stories Sid had told me and the stories I'd heard in other western places seem hauntingly alike.

That question led me to a large-scale search for oral narratives in the West, of which this book is the ultimate product. Doing the research meant a series of trips out West over a period of four years. Each time I left the Midwest for the West, I was exhilarated: I loved nothing better than immersing myself in a landscape that offered such a contrast to where I had been living for the past dozen years. And each time I had to head the car east again, my spirits sank. Each time it became harder to do. I finally identified the sinking feeling as homesickness for the West, spawned by the stories I was collecting and the landscapes I was traveling through. At the time I was troubled by this feeling, as though I had no right to be homesick for a place that wasn't technically home for me.

The stories were making me homesick, I eventually realized, because they were infused with a sense of place, connecting the people who told the stories with the places in which the tellers lived. I longed for that kind of connection myself. In the process of putting this book together, the stories have afforded me a way of making that connection vicariously, of seeing that it can be made, of discovering that a connection with place is essential to becoming fully human. And stories are one vehicle, a powerful one, for doing so—all the more powerful perhaps because they transcend individual experience and become communal expressions of those connections.

So I am finally coming to understand what Sid wanted me to see: that a place lives for us, that we belong to it most fully, that we find ourselves in place, when we know it through stories, including our own, and when we pass those stories on to others. Only when we come to understand ourselves as belonging to a place (rather than a place belonging to us) can we begin to take care of it.

———— ❧ ————

In *The Stars, the Snow, the Fire: Twenty-five Years in the Alaska Wilderness* (New York, 1992), John Haines writes about a part of Alaska that he came to know as a homesteader and trapper in the 1950s. Each time he made a circuit of his trap-lines, the places he visited grew richer with meaning, imbued with memories of the experiences he'd had at each spot. The trails he followed "acquired their home legend of past kills and other memorable events.... In a few seasons the country became worn and familiar like a neighborhood."

The land Haines traversed became a kind of geography of the soul. "The physical domain of the country had its counterpart in me," he writes. "The trails I made led outward into the hills and swamps, but they led inward also. And from the study of things underfoot, and from reading and thinking, came a kind of exploration, myself and the land. In time the two became one in my mind."

In counterpoint to his direct experience of the land were the stories Haines heard from other, older trappers in the area, stories of danger, loneliness, and survival. The cabins and trails, rivers and ridges that figured in these stories resonated for Haines with new meaning when he saw them after hearing the stories.

The process that Haines describes is how place and landscape acquire meaning, how we come to feel a link with the land on which we live and within which we move, how we derive a sense of belonging to and identity with a place and the familiar contours of its landscape. This process, as Haines suggests, has two components: our direct experience of a place and the sharing of that experience in story form. Such stories make connections between places and moments. We can make a place our own, imbue it with memories, through our own experiences there. But relying on these alone to give a place meaning leaves us unconnected with other people who have seen and known and loved or feared or loathed it. To hear a story about a place is to expand our own perception of the place, to deepen its meaning beyond our own experience. Hearing others' stories about a place enriches us by letting us participate vicariously in their experiences, extending our sense of place not only beyond ourselves, but even beyond our own lifetimes.

To share a place through story is to find a bond that cannot be broken while the place is there. As we tell and listen to stories about a place, we come to understand its effects on us, how its weather, its shapes and scents, its patterns of light and shadow, its colors and forms have imprinted us with that sense of familiarity that makes us call it home and makes us feel as though we somehow belong there. And belong as well to the human communities in the past that have also called it home.

The stories in this book attest to that process. They are told by Anglo westerners, some of them long-time residents of the region, others recent arrivals. In one way or another, all of the stories are about how people find a place for themselves in the West, how they are shaped by the place, and how they construct an identity for themselves as a result. And the stories are evidence of how the experience of place has been communicated to others to become part of the shared knowledge and communal understanding of the place. The stories describe migration to the region, encounters with and responses to its natural environment, and the shaping of identity as a result of these experiences. These do not represent all the kinds or subjects of stories that Anglos tell, by any means. Nor is it meant to. My purpose in selecting and telling these stories here is to suggest how the regional identity of a particular group of people is shaped around the experience of place.

The stories are drawn from a corpus of more than a thousand narrative texts that I assembled in the course of my research. Some come from my own fieldwork, others from conversations with western friends, but the bulk are from folklore, oral history, and local history collections found in university libraries, state and local historical societies, and state libraries and archives in eleven western states. In making the selections of texts to be included here, I have tried to present a cross-section of stories from throughout the region to show that the relationship between place and identity is endemic to the American West. And I have included stories from the end of the nineteenth century up through the present to suggest that the process of making connections with place is a continual and continuing one.

The texts that I gathered dealt with innumerable topics and reflected myriad themes. To make some sense of the collection as a coherent expression of the western regional experience, I looked for overall patterns linking the stories to one another in a coherent way, patterns that suggested the presence of a larger Story underlying the individual texts. At the same time that I was engaged in this search, I was also undergoing profound changes in my personal life that involved, among other things, moving out West where I hoped, after half a lifetime of wandering, to find myself finally in place. Preoccupied as I was with this process, it is no surprise that I began to see it reflected in the stories I was dealing with. By coming to understand that the stories dealt less with the past than with place and with the shaping of identity around place, I began to perceive the Story behind the stories: that place has the power to shape identity. There are doubtless other story lines contained in the collection, other ways of linking topics and themes together into larger narrative structures. But the Story of how people come to find themselves in place and to belong to it is the story that most appeals to me at this moment, and it is the Story that the stories in this book are arranged to tell.

As a collection of oral narratives, the book is intended as a contribution to the regional literature of the western United States, a literature in which the landscape plays a critical role and the relationship between the land and its residents is a dominant theme. The stories presented here represent a rich vein of oral literature, a vein that is virtually invisible in discussions of western literature and history—undeservedly so because this oral narrative tradition, like other forms of vernacular culture, expresses the genuine experiences of westerners and articulates clearly their values and beliefs and sense of themselves *as* westerners. A consideration of western vernacular culture seems especially needed at this moment when the West is being redefined by western historians and literary critics.

Perhaps the most difficult task of all in this endeavor has been to translate the power of the spoken word, the told story, into printed form, to present the stories in a way that does justice to their nature as the creative expressions of living, breathing human beings. To do so I have had to abandon the role of analyst and take on the role of performer, to become myself the voice through which the stories can tell themselves. I do so in all humility, in an attempt to communicate the meaning and power and beauty and effect of the stories as I imagine they were in their tellings. This has rarely been easy, for many of the texts I found in the archives were too long or too brief, too awkward or stilted, to be recognizable as stories that had been orally told. But they struck me nonetheless as somehow having lives of their own despite the shrouds in which they were wrapped. I retell them here in the spirit of bringing them back to life, casting myself in the role of storyteller entering the stream of tradition from which the stories came, retelling the stories, as each storyteller must, to suit the purpose and audience of the moment. They have rolled around in my head long enough, it seems, for the unnecessary details to have worn away and the essence of each story to become apparent on the polished surface.

I believe that stories live beyond the original occasions on which they were told, that they can speak to us of the universals of human experience, that they can cause us to reflect on our own experiences, that these stories in particular can speak to our own sense of place and our own identities as shaped by the places in which we live. I want these stories to awaken in you the necessity for telling stories that connect us with place by recounting the human experiences, our own and others', that have taken place there. If they have that effect on you, then I have done them justice.

PART ONE
Coming into the Country

The Story begins with origins:
How did westerners come to be where they are?

Coming into the Country

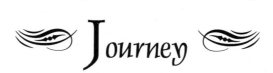

Journey

FOR THE STORYTELLERS, western origins lie in a journey from an old home to a new one, a journey that marks the emergence of a new identity.

All journeys have beginnings and endings, but these are barely limned in most of the stories. Little is said of where people came from, and only a few of the travelers reach their destinations by the end of their stories. The focus instead is on the process of getting there, on the dangers encountered, the hardships endured along the way for the sake of the goal that is sought. The trail becomes the venue for a rite of passage in which identity is transformed.

As omnipresent elements in these stories, danger and hardship, along with the threat or fact of death, suggest that the ultimate goal of the journey is not to be won without risk, without sacrifice; if it were, it would be worthless. Some blood must be paid to the gods of metamorphosis. But none of these stories is without triumph of some kind, or else the story itself would not be told by survivors. And, implicitly or explicitly, each of the stories points to the present as a reason to recount the past. We would not be who we are, where we are, the storytellers say, if our ancestors had not done what they did to get here.

MY GRANDFATHER TOOK off from Ohio in 1849, I believe.

Left there, and got here in 1850.
He came with a wagon train,
but he had to give the captain of the train so much

2/6/1999 sunday
JUst STARF!!
Salt Lake City
trip

F rom: Bob Nasworth
Bought in
Sept. - October
1998
at:
Ft. Bredger
dc 1825 Wyoming
border oran
Utah Hugh, 1-80

received today 2/6/1999
1998
Belated christmas
gift

for the privilege of traveling with him,
   besides driving an ox team.
So when he landed here,
  all he had was a rifle,
  and a frying pan,
  and a buffalo robe,
   besides the clothes he stood in.
That's the way he got west,
  walked every doggone step of the way
   from St. Joe, Missouri,
    to Weaverville
     up here in Trinity County.

California

MY GREAT-GRANDMOTHER was a very stubborn woman.
She and her husband had loaded up their wagon
  and started to come west.
But when they got to the point
  where they joined up with a wagon company
   and were about to cross the Missouri,
my great-grandfather decided
  they would have to lighten the wagon.
So he told her she would have to leave
  her beautiful copper kettle
   and her big feather mattress.
But she had already had to give up most of her household goods;
  these were all that she had left,
   and she refused to leave them behind.
So he took the kettle and the mattress out of the wagon
  and laid them by the side of the road.
She sat right down beside them
  and said that she wasn't going without them.
   If they stayed behind, so would she.
So the men took the wagons and drove off,
  and she stayed there.
Then, after a while, he relented,

and turned their wagon around
    and came back to get her.
They decided she could take the kettle *and* the mattress
    if she emptied out the feathers.
Because she could always fill the tick with new feathers
    when they settled a new place.

Washington

WHEN MY GRANDMOTHER came out here,
    she had a piano.
Grandfather met her in Pueblo
    and they got married.
She had inherited a houseful of furniture
    and she wanted to have it shipped out here.
But Grandfather said he didn't think
    they could afford to have it all sent out.
So he told her,
    "You pick one piece.
    We'll have that sent out."
So she picked the piano.
So they shipped that out
    and that was supposed to be the first piano
        in the San Luis Valley.

Colorado

MY FAMILY TRAVELED BY rail from New York to Chicago.
    By then the railroad went all the way to Laramie.
But there were no Pullmans or chaircars available.
So from Chicago to Laramie,
    they rode in a boxcar,
    and the doors were all closed up
        until they felt like they would suffocate.
So my father found a crowbar
    and broke through the door of the car,
    and that let them get some fresh air.

Utah

20 *Coming into the Country*

MY GRANDFATHER was converted to the Mormon church
　　in Denmark.
When the time was right, he came to America.
He joined the Willie Handcart Company,
　　which, as you know, got started late.
You can read in the history books
　　about the terrible things they suffered.
He lost his only son
　　and a little daughter.
His feet froze and finally got so bad
　　　that his wife either had to pull him in the handcart
　　　　or leave him behind.
Well, he pleaded with her to leave him,
　　but she couldn't do it.
　　She would never do it.
So he was put in the handcart and hauled for miles.

Finally, the relief party came,
　　and he survived.
But his feet were always crooked after that.
　　The Indians called him "Crooked Feet."

Utah

MY GREAT-GRANDMOTHER came across the plains as a little girl.
Of course, they traveled with a wagon train.
One night on the trail,
　　　when the wagon company was in Wyoming,
　　the weather was especially bad
　　　and the temperature that night
　　　　went way below zero.
So my great-grandmother slept next to another little girl.

When they woke up the next morning,
　　they found that the other little girl had frozen to death,
　　and my great-grandmother's long hair

was frozen to her body.
The only way to get them apart was to cut off her hair.

My aunt still has the pair of scissors they used.
Utah

———— ❧ ————

THERE'S AN OLD GRAVE on our ranch
    on the side of the hill toward the bottom.
When I first moved there,
    I noticed this little picket fence on the side of the hill.
It was kind of grown over
    with dried sagebrush and weeds around it,
but I could see that it was definitely a marker for something.

Later I was told—I can't remember who by,
    maybe it was the old man who owned the grocery store
        on Main Street—
    that a child was buried there.
This family had come across the rimrock in a covered wagon
    and the little girl had gotten sick,
        so they were forced to camp there for the night.
But she died.
So they buried her there alongside the hill
    to preserve the grave,
        instead of out on the flat
    where it probably would have become lost
        in time.
They put a little picket fence around the grave
    to mark it,
        and it's still there to this day.
Oregon

———— ❧ ————

MY FATHER AND HIS FAMILY lived in the little town of Gorham,
Maine, near Portland. In about 1898 he came out to Wyoming at
the invitation of his older brother who had already homesteaded
a ranch on the north fork of the Shoshone River above Cody. And

my father selected a plot of land as a homestead just about three miles above this ranch on the same river. He built cabins and an irrigation ditch there.

Then, in 1900, he arranged for our family—my mother, two older sisters, and myself—to come out here to settle with him on this homestead. We traveled on the train, and it took about a week to make the trip from Maine out to the town of Red Lodge, Montana, which was the nearest railroad point to our new home there in Cody.

We landed there at Red Lodge in June of 1900. And my father was there from Cody to meet us and take us down to the homestead. He had a team of horses and a ranch wagon, and we loaded our gear that we had brought on the train into the wagon and we children sat on board seats in the back of the wagon, with my mother and father in front. It took us three or four days to get from Red Lodge out to the homestead, quite a trip in those days.

We had to cross the south fork of the Shoshone River, which was in high water at that time. It was kind of a dangerous crossing, and he didn't want us to attempt to cross in the wagon. So my uncle Charles had arranged with the neighbors to stretch a cable across the river and had a cage attached to it. And that was supposed to be our way of getting across the river with the family. The team of horses and the wagon that we were in managed to cross the river by fording lower down.

My older sister, Martha, was the first person to be pulled across in this cage. And about midway across, why, the cage dipped way down into the water. My mother was in hysterics, you know, standing on the bank there, watching it. But they managed to pull the cage back to the same side again. And my uncle, who was over on the other side, managed to tighten the cable and so we started out again and got across, got the family across safely. And we got to the homestead that day.

About two weeks later my father went back to Red Lodge with his team and wagon to pick up the furniture that had been shipped out from Maine. On the last day of his trip back from there, he had stopped over the hill from Red Lodge at noon to rest his horses and feed them some grain. And while he was doing that, a band of Indians who had been celebrating in the town of Red Lodge came up over the hill all dressed in their colorful regalia and whooping and hollering, and it frightened the team of horses. And they turned and knocked my father down on the ground and trampled over him and pulled the wagon over him and fatally wounded him. They picked him up, the Indians did, and took him back into Red Lodge. But he only lived until the next day.

So they called my mother and one of the neighbors took her up there. He was buried in a little cemetery in the town of Red Lodge. And his body is still there. But the grave had a wooden marker and sometime later a grass fire burned the marker down and also the cemetery house and they lost the records. And we never knew, we don't know to this day just what particular plot of ground my father was buried in.

Wyoming

※

THIS YOUNG MOTHER in one of the wagon trains
    had a very sick baby.
And, of course, there was no medicine, no doctor,
    no help at all.
She begged the people to stop
    until the baby got better
but they were afraid of Indians and wanted to keep going.

Finally, the baby died,
    but they wouldn't even stop to let her bury it right.

So the mother wrapped the baby up,
    set the little body in the sand,
        and piled brush and rocks around it,
            to keep the animals away.

But that night, she couldn't sleep
    for thinking about wild animals and Indians.
So she got up, got on a horse, and went back to find the body.

It took her most of the night.
When she finally found it,
    she leaned over and heard the baby breathing.
    And when she opened the covers, it cried!

Now that baby was my great-grandmother.
Utah

—❧—

THERE WAS A party of settlers
    coming across the northern route into Oregon
        in the Columbia Basin
        in the middle of winter.
All the way, they disputed
    whether to travel by horse or by canoe.
And the party split up over it, split in two.

But both groups got into desperate straits.
    They got lost.
    They were forced to drink their own urine.
    For food they had just one beaver
    to share among seven people.

When half of the party was down to their last horse,
    they saw the other half on the other side of the river,
        on their last legs,
            looking like apparitions through the mist.
So they killed their last horse,
    made a canoe out of its hide
    and carried the horsemeat
        over to the other side of the river.

Oregon

—❧—

MY GRANDFATHER AND THESE two other men with him
    were looking for land.
    They just kept coming north,
    didn't stop to do any mining.
They were looking for land.

It was in the winter time,
  and crossing Mad River
    they lost their pack mule with all their food on it,
    and snow on the ground.
So they kept heading this way, and they come to a place
  where some folks had started to carry supplies
    into the mines from Humboldt Bay.
And it had got to be winter
  so they had built this lean-to or cache
  and stored the things that they had there,
    which was flour and eggs.

Well, my grandfather and these other men found this cache.
And one man had on an army overcoat
  with a lot of padding in the shoulders.
So he took some of that padding out
  and fired his pistol through there
  and got it on fire
  and got a fire built that way.
Then they took their ramrods
  and made a dough by opening a sack of flour
    and breaking half a dozen eggs in there—
      which weren't very good by then—
    and stirred it around
    until they got a gob of that dough on their ramrods
    and then stuck it in the fire.
  It made them awful sick
    but it kept them from starving to death
      until they killed some game
      and then they were all right.
California

———— ❧ ————

BEFORE THEY left Denmark,
  Krestine got pregnant.
After a week on the ship
  she was morning sick *and* seasick.

26 *Coming into the Country*

The ladies on the ship did their best to help her,
but she said she prayed daily.
        One day she'd pray to die,
        and the next day she'd pray to live.

They got to New York,
        stayed there a few months,
Then joined a wagon train to Nevada,
        where the new homestead was.
Got to Reno, rested there a week or so.

Then Granddad borrowed a wagon and team
        and loaded it with sugar, flour, beans, and bacon,
and early one morning they set out for the ranch.
She had never seen it;
        all she did was hear him rave about it.
They rode all day across sagebrush and sand
        and through the junipers over rough terrain—
                no road, just a wagon trail.

Just before dusk
        on the top of the hill (that we call the sandhill),
he stopped the wagon,
        and he looked down.
His eyes were just shining.
He looked down over the meadow,
        so happy and proud,
and he said, "Krestine, *this* is it."
She looked up at him,
        she was so tired and sick and all of it together.
And she said,
        "Sophus, this is the last place, isn't it?
        There is no beyond, is there?"

Nevada

———— ❧ ————

WHEN THE IMMIGRANTS, including the Thomases, finally reached
their destination, they poured out of the wagons. The men set

out to arrange the camp, while the women began to unpack their few remaining treasures from the Old World, pieces of furniture and family china that had miraculously escaped being broken during the long hard trek.

While the adults were getting settled in, little Mary Ann Thomas decided to climb a pine tree to play scout. But when she climbed back down, she was covered with pitch. It had gotten in her hair, and she cried as her mother tried to comb it out.

Finally it became clear that the only thing to do was to cut her hair—the beautiful black curls that had been the pride of her grandfather, whom they had left in Wales. He would certainly have disapproved had he seen his daughter and grandchildren, who had been brought up amid the charm of Old World customs, now living in the wild West.

Montana

———— ❦ ————

GRANDMA COULD NEVER understand
    why anyone would want to cultivate a cactus.
She and her husband had walked across the plains as children,
    through thorny weeds and rocks.
Grandpa said his feet were torn and bleeding,
    so that many times
        he could hardly walk.
His mother tried to keep the family clean,
    but his feet had healed with dirt still under the skin.

When he died of cancer at age 67,
    my father stood by his bed.
The nurse said,
    "I wonder why the bottoms of his feet are black."
My father said,
    "It is all right.
    He is carrying the soil of the plains with him,
        even to his grave."

Utah

Coming into the Country

~ Encounter ~

THOSE WHO COME West often have no clear idea of what they will find, only images shaped by their desires. They come for different purposes, some eagerly, others reluctantly, at the mercy of another's dream. And some are just passing through. The place affects them all in different ways, arouses a range of emotions in them, as they bring their expectations to bear on what they see, their expectations not just of the place but of themselves and of how life might be lived there. What they find is a place that is subversive of expectations, resistant to desires, a force to be reckoned with. In the stories, the western landscape is a presence that cannot be ignored, that always evokes a response, that often calls for action, that sometimes poses a psychic threat. So in these stories are elation and astonishment, horror and disgust, humor and wonder and anxiety—but never indifference.

JOHNSON WAS THE first man that came on down this inlay here.
When they was coming down through Portas Pass,
    they camped over there in the pass out here.
He lost his oxen, and he landed out on the hill.
He came out on the top of that hill—
    and it struck him so because he'd come on it
        all of a sudden.
Looked down over the valley—
    spring of the year and it was green—
He throwed out his arms,
    and said, "Mine by discovery."
Utah

30

WELL, I HAD ASTHMA very badly.
And the doctor,
     our physician,
          was very concerned about me.
And he suggested that my family pick up and move out West
     where the atmosphere was a little cleaner.
So Chicago apparently must have been —
     the air must have been contaminated
          in those days.
So we took the train out.
And on the way out on the train,
     my two older brothers said,
          "Oh, we're going to coast down those mountains
               when we get to them this winter."

And when we got to the Rockies,
     we looked at those jagged rocky peaks.
They changed their minds a bit
     and tempered it,
          "Well, we'll slide down the foothills, probably."

Colorado

I MOVED HERE from New York last year,
     drove across country.
And when I got to Denver,
those mountains just got to me somehow.
So I rolled down the window and screamed at them,
     "I am important,
      I am important."

California

AFTER MY PARENTS were married,
     they came to Laramie to live.
When my mother saw Pilot Knob,
     she said to my father,
          "Oh, let's walk over to that pretty hill up there."

She thought it was just a short distance away,
    that they could walk up there.
But it was actually several miles.
So she early learned that seeing things here
    was different from seeing things in Illinois,
    that the climate had an effect on your eyes
        and what you saw.

Wyoming

I HAVE TO TELL a funny joke.
My father and another man, his cousin,
    were homesteading land over in Timnath
        which is right inside the town of Timnath now.
And a young fellow come along,
    hitchhiking.
He wanted to know if they had any work for him to do.
So they told him to stay a while
    and help them with the farm work.

One morning,
    I think one Sunday morning,
        he got up early and said,
            "I'm going to hike over to those foothills.
        But I'll be back for breakfast."

My father and his cousin,
    they exchanged glances,
        but they didn't say anything at all.
Well, he came back
    just as the sun was setting,
        tired,
        dirty,
        and hungry.
"Why in the world
    didn't you tell me
        how deceiving those mountains were?"

Colorado

Coming into the Country

GRANDFATHER WAS MUCH older than Grandmother.
When she came here to live at this house,
    after they were married,
        he used to go down in the fields there
            to hay and whatever he had to do,
    and she would walk out to meet him.
She said those mountains were just *pressing* her *down.*
    They made her feel terrible.
She just knew the rolling hills in Illinois.
She didn't like these big mountains at all,
    when she first got here.
But later she loved them.

Nevada

I WAS DRIVING through southern Utah on the way to Nevada with a friend of mine from Kentucky. And I don't know if you've ever been through there, but the road goes through the Virgin River Gorge which is real narrow and winding, with big cliffs on either side.

Well, we're driving along and all of a sudden, the road comes around a curve at the end of the canyon and it opens out onto the desert, with mountains way in the distance, and you can see practically all the way to Las Vegas from there. So I said, "Wow! Look! You can see forever." And he looked and then he got pale and broke out in a cold sweat, and told me to stop the car. So I pulled over to the side of the road, and he opened the door, swung his feet out, and just sat and stared at the ground for a few minutes.

After we got back on the road, going across that valley, he just kept his eyes to the side of the road or inside the car. All that distance and space unnerved him because he was used to Kentucky, with rolling hills and trees where you can't see very far in any one direction.

California

I HAD TO FLY FROM Denver to Rock Springs for the job interview
    on this little puddle jumper.
        Nineteen seats —
            I counted them.

So we're on this plane,
    bouncing around,
        and the captain comes on the P.A. system and says,
        "This is the captain speaking.
        We're thirty-seven miles from Rock Springs.
        The temperature is forty-one degrees.
        Visibility is thirty-five miles.
        We'll be touching down in eight minutes."
I look out the window,
    and it's just beautiful.
You can see the Rockies
    just strewn across the world
        with little tufts of clouds.

So we land at the Rock Springs airport,
    the door opens,
        and the whole plane rocks with the impact of the wind
            that's blowing snow through the door!
To get out the damn door
    you have to grab both sides with your hands
        and pull yourself out!

Well, the pilot was standing right next to the stairs
    as I got out.
And I turned around to him and I said,
    "You lied!"
And he said,
    "No, I didn't.
    Eight minutes ago it was true.
    Welcome to Wyoming!"
Wyoming

WELL, IT WAS raining.
>You know how it looks in Ouray.
And it was raining,
>and the ground was covered with stumps and logs,
>>and it was very gloomy.

This woman on the stage with me
>looked out from the back of the wagon.
And I remember that distinctly.
>Her face was powdered with starch
>>and she was very ghastly looking.
>She had a beautiful complexion and she took care of it.
And she said,
>"I'm just as disappointed as ever I can be."

Colorado

———

THEN THERE WAS the bachelor
>who had settled on the creek along a stage route
>and they established a post office in his log house.
He was the postmaster
>and they called the post office by his last name.

Well, he joined one of those Heart and Hand marriage clubs
>and got to corresponding with a woman,
>>"Object: matrimony."
In his correspondence
>he told her that he owned a whole town,
>>every building in it,
>>and it was named after him.

Well, they became engaged
>and he was to meet her at the railroad town
>>at a certain time.
Well, they met and were married
>and the next day drove out to the ranch.
She kept asking him how much farther it was
>and he told her not much farther.

So eventually they came over a hill in sight of the creek
       and the little log house
       and a little shed or so.
And he said, "There it is.
       I own the whole town,
           every building in it."

She went back to town on the next stage.

Montana

THERE WAS A man and woman,
       sitting at a table in this restaurant.
My husband knew them
       and we sat down at their table.
He told them how homesick I was.
       I thought it was an awful place.
The lady said,
       "The longer she stays here, the worse it will be."
She said,
       "Any man that would bring a woman to this place
           should get down on his knees three times a day."
You can imagine how I felt.

But after I'd been home,
       back to Massachusetts two or three times,
I was perfectly contented to live out here.

New Mexico

MY MOTHER LOOKED at all the sagebrush and said to my father, "Golly, wouldn't it be nice if I could wave a wand and all that sagebrush would disappear?"

    He said, "Yes, it would. That is what happens. The only thing is you have to wave that wand a good many times." He meant the grubbing hoe.

Utah

Learning to Live with the Land

Once arrived,
according to the Story, the newcomer finds
that the place is neither welcoming nor comfortable.

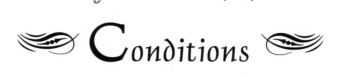

Learning to Live with the Land

Conditions

S ETTLING IN MEANS COMING to terms with the land itself, the environmental conditions that prevail there. In the West, the most fundamental of these is the presence or absence, amount and quality of water. So storytellers describe the difficulties of obtaining water in the West, which can be, literally, a matter of life or death. Over and over the storytellers measure the cost of water in human life.

Scarce water means sparse settlement, with people scattered across the landscape, living on isolated ranches and farmsteads sometimes miles from their nearest neighbor. In this human landscape, company is nearly as precious a commodity as water.

Survival under these conditions depends on cooperation and generosity, a sense of fellow feeling among those sharing the empty, arid places together.

ONE OF THE FIRST EXPLORING parties through east central Montana followed the Musselshell north to its junction with the Missouri at Fort Musselshell. In crossing the Musselshell River to the east bank they made a serious mistake because the streams east of there were very few and far between.

The party got two or three days' journey from the Musselshell when their water was exhausted and they began to suffer from thirst. They turned back toward the Musselshell, but they were still a day's journey away when they came across a pool of stagnant water in which there were swarms of little red worms. The men were so desperate for a drink of water that they hunted around till they found some fairly long grass straws that were hollow. They stuck the straws deep down through the worms into the water in an effort to get enough water to drink to keep from perishing of thirst. But the effects of the water were almost as bad as the thirst itself, as they all got sick from the colic-morgus.

Montana

───── ❧ ─────

IN 1887, I WAS HEADED across the Llano Estacado from Texas to New Mexico. I had two small barrels with me that I filled with water every time I came to a watering place. The first two days of the trip were just as pleasant as could be. The days were warm and the wind was calm. The nights were cool and the stars were the brightest that I had ever seen.

But on the morning of the third day a sand storm rolled up. It was clear and bright when I broke camp that morning, but I could see a red haze in the west, and by ten o'clock I could not see the road and the horses could not face the wind. This kept up for two days and nights, and I realized that the water in the barrels was giving out. On the morning of the third day the wind had just about blown itself out, so I set off again. I had lost all sense of direction except that I knew I was going in a westerly direction. I do not know how far I traveled that day. Next morning I found that the water had nearly all leaked out of the barrels, but I harnessed my horses and traveled until they gave out. It was very hot—a blazing sun and no breeze.

The next day there was no water or no food either for me or the horses. To make things worse, another sand storm came up and I couldn't see anything. It soon passed on, and about two o'clock, I suppose, I rested the team, with no grass, no feed, no water. I found a dry biscuit in my grub box, and drained a cup of water from the barrel. I sat down on the opposite side of the wagon from my horses to eat and drink for I could not bear to look at them.

While I was sitting there, a mockingbird appeared and perched on the side of my cup. It took a drink, then flew off toward the west. I decided to follow the bird, hoping it would lead me to water. I came across a trail leading in the direction the bird had gone and followed it as fast as the horses could travel. I saw a mirage in front of me, and I dared not take my eyes off it. I think the horses saw it too. We had traveled about six miles, when the mirage changed into a reality, for we could see the tops of trees and then a bank or cliff covered with trees and shrubs. So we came to the edge of a canyon and on the other side were the green trees, with water trickling out of the bank underneath them. It flowed into a rock-lined lake.

I tested the water to make sure it was safe for the horses because I had heard that in some parts of the West the water was alkali and would kill the stock, but here it was as clear as crystal. As I sat there resting, the mockingbird reappeared, and I silently thanked it for saving me when I was so near death.

New Mexico

A COUPLE OF COWBOYS were out on a trail herd
    for two days without water.
Finally they found a very small pond
    and the cattle rushed into it for water.
One of the cowboys jumped down among the cattle
    and started to drink the muddy water.
The other one went around to the other side of the pond
    and called to his partner,
        "Why don't you come up here
            where the water is clear?"
The first cowboy said,
        "It doesn't make a damn bit of difference.
            I'm going to drink her dry anyhow."

Wyoming

MRS. STEWART WAS TRAVELING with her children
    from Moapa to Las Vegas.
They had filled a fifty-gallon tank of water
    and fastened it under the wagon.

They started out at four o'clock in the morning
    and made good time.
When they had come about twenty miles from Moapa
    and were still thirty miles from Vegas,
        they stopped to make camp for the night.
But when they went to get water for themselves and their horses,
    the water was gone!
The stopper had come out
    and the jolting of the wagon had spilt all the water
        from the tank.
There they were in the middle of the desert,
    with no trees or shade
        and not a drop of water to be had
            within thirty miles.
There was nothing to be done but rest overnight.
    So Mrs. Stewart and the children lay down
        and went to sleep.
When they woke up,
    they felt a little better
        after the cool desert night.
They decided to go on,
    but the horses soon gave out.

The only thing to be done
    was for the Stewart boy to go for help.
So he saddled a pony that had been tied behind the wagon
    and so was in a little better condition.
He rode and rode and kept prodding his horse to go on.
When he reached the ranch, the horse dropped.
The boy slid off and went stumbling in.
The people there guessed from his appearance
    what was the matter,
and hurried to fill a water tank and harness a team.
When he was able to talk, he told them where to go.
With the fresh horses from the ranch,
    the rescue party managed to reach the Stewarts just at dusk.
Nevada

MY FOLKS HAD ONE of the early ranches in here,
  and it was kind of a way station on the trail.
My father had dug a shallow well there
  which barely furnished enough water for us.
I remember one day a big train of transient people come along.
Oh, they had dogs and horses and cattle.
  They was movin' somewhere up above
    and they stopped for water
      and my father wasn't there.
And he'd said,
  "Agnes, give 'em all the water they want to drink."
He said,
  "Don't ever refuse 'em a drink of water
    or their kegs to take with them,
but we can't furnish the stock water," he said.
  "Because we haven't got it."
When we dipped it, it was muddy.

So they come along and I told them, I said,
  "Well, go out and get what you want to drink
    and fill up your kegs,
  but don't try to water your stock
    'cause we haven't got it."
I said,
  "It gets to be muddy so we can't use it."
So they didn't pay any attention to me at all
  and they said, "Well, we're gonna water our stock."
I said,
  "No, you're not gonna water your stock."
I said,
  "I think it's kindness enough of us
    to give you all you want to drink
      and to let you fill your kegs,
  but we cannot furnish you water for stock."

So they went to pullin' water up outa the well
        to water the stock
and there was a gun sittin' beside the door
    and I picked the gun up and I said,
        "Now listen,
            you are not watering that stock.
Now," I said, "move on.
        You've got all the water you can use,
                you've got your kegs full,
                        and you cannot water that stock."
Well, they went on.
        I guess they thought they had to.

Well, he eventually dug a couple more wells
        and that give plenty of water for the stockmen
                and for the freighters
                        and everybody to have plenty of water.
But we never charged any of them a cent for water.
        Pa wouldn't do it.
He said he didn't think it was right
        to charge people for water
and he wouldn't do it.
New Mexico

<hr />

WE WERE ON OUR way through Nevada.
At one place on that trip where we stopped,
        there was a clay formation in the soil
                and the fellow had a well dug.
It was probably only ten feet or so down to water.
And, of course,
        we carried two barrels,
                a barrel on each side of each wagon
                        with water to use.
        You didn't always know just what you'd find
                at the next stop in traveling.
And the old fella said,

"The well is right over there,
　　　You're welcome to all the water you want," he said,
　　"But you'll have to use a pole
　　　　because a mare's colt fell in yesterday
　　　　　　and I haven't figured how to get it out."
It drowned in the well.
He said by pushing it over to one side
　　　you could tip out a bucket of water.
Sounds hard to tell it.
　　　You kind of lose your taste for water.
Well, that was an actual happening.
　　　I saw the colt in the well
　　　　　　when I got close enough to look over.

Nevada

———— ❧ ————

WHEN I FIRST SAW New Mexico,
　　　it was in 1904.
We came here from Omaha
　　　and we had to go to El Paso to get the train
　　　　　　to go to Prescott, Arizona.
And, of course, we were all girls and we were all thirsty.
In the train station there at El Paso,
　　　they had one of those five-gallon things in the corner,
so we got some water,
　　　and we spit it out.
　　　　　Oh, it was terrible.
My father was embarrassed by the way we acted,
　　　so he walked up there,
　　　　　a big man, you know,
　　　and he took a drink.
What *we* said was nothing to what *he* said.
He said,
　　"For God's sake,
　　　　you mean to say that humans drink this stuff?"
We found that we could buy mineral water.
　　　I think it was five cents a glass.

And it cost my father about three dollars to give us all a drink.
He said, "Wait 'til we get out of this country."
New Mexico

―――――

I'LL HAVE TO TELL you a big laugh that we had.
You can tell that we were on edge
    living like we were,
and lots of times we'd laugh to keep from crying,
    laugh and cry together.

But anyway, we had these barrels here
    and we'd fill 'em with snow water.
We'd melt the tub full of water,
    then put it into the barrels
        and melt another tub full of water.
Do that to get these barrels all filled.

Then we wanted to draw some water out of the barrels
    and neither one of us had learned very well
        how to draw the water out of these barrels.
And Aunt Doretta, she said,
    "I can't do it, I can't."
And I said, "I can.
    Give it to me."
And I was trying to draw
    and I couldn't draw it,
and I lay down on my back,
    put my feet up on the barrels
        and give a big suck on that hose—
and I got the water!
    About choked to death.
And then we laughed and bawled and laughed and bawled,
    laughed at me getting my mouth full
        and bawled because we wasted it!"
Utah

―――――

EVERY DAY FOR A YEAR he walked a mile for his coffee can of water. When people asked why he didn't drill a well for himself, he said that he was afraid it was just as far one way to water as the other.

Oregon

THE BRIGGS BROTHERS WERE digging a well on their place
      about a mile east of us.
When the well was about sixty feet deep,
       the horse they were using to pull the bucket up
          got excited and backed into the well.
Ray was down there.
      When he tried to climb up the rope
         to get past the horse,
            they both fell to the bottom together.
His brother John got hysterical
      and wanted to climb down after him,
         but we kept him from that.
We decided the only thing to do was for someone to climb down
      and cut the horse up,
         haul up the pieces,
           and get the man out.
When we finally got the horse out,
      Ray was buried in the mud at the bottom of the well.
         We put a cable around his waist
           and pulled his body out,
             his shoes still stuck in the mud.

We later heard the rumor that his hair had turned white,
      but that was not true.
But I sometimes wonder why some of us didn't turn gray
      that night.
Now, sixty years later, I drive along the highway
      almost every day
and pass within a hundred feet of the site
      although there's nothing there now to mark the spot.

And I wonder how anyone could have said,
    "The land is free."

Idaho

GRANDDAD MOREY WAS the justice of the peace,
    and Granddad Masters dug himself a ditch.
He was out in the field irrigating
    and the water quit,
        so he went up to the head of the ditch
            and there was a hole in the dam.
So he fixed it, and went on down and irrigated a little while
    and pretty soon the water quit again.
And he went back up—
    it was about a mile and a half
        up to the head of the ditch—
    and he walked up there,
    and here was a hole in the ditch again.
So he fixed it, and went on down the ditch a little ways,
    then cut off through the brush,
        circled around and came back.
Pretty soon, an old fellow who lived up the creek there,
    come sneaking out there
        and started poking this hole in the ditch,
so Granddad walked out there,
    and he had the shovel with him,
        so he just hauled off
            and peeled him with the shovel
                and knocked him cold.
He come on down home and got on his horse
    and come over to Granddad Morey
        and said he wanted to pay his fine for the assault.
So Granddad Morey fined him five bucks,
    and he paid,
and he hadn't much more than got out of sight
    'til here come this fellow's wife,

that got knocked cold.
She wanted a warrant sworn out
for "that mean old man Masters."
He'd hit her husband in the side of the head with a shovel
and "knocked him sensible."
Granddad Morey laughed about that until the day he died.
He said she'd never said a truer word in her life.

Utah

THE LAST CHANCE DITCH Company was organized in 1895. It seems that the early homesteaders had tried everything to get their places irrigated and it had all failed. This ditch was the last hope, so they called it the Last Chance. It was sort of a desperation attempt, and I don't think many of the farmers thought it would work, but it was tried and worked in a sort of haphazard way. Some of the local men say it is the only ditch in the state where water runs uphill.

Well, since 1895 the ditch company has been in one lawsuit after another. The one that stands out in my mind happened about ten years ago. One of the oldtimers in the community, Ole Hetland, was on the stand testifying as to whether waste water from the Last Chance had washed out the Bartlett ditch. Well, on the stand he was asked by the lawyer for the Bartlett, if it was possible for water to get from the Last Chance to the Bartlett. And Ole replied that there was one way he knew of. So the lawyer thought he saw a way to break the case and he asked Ole how this could be done. Ole, who is an old country Norwegian, replied in broken English that the only way he knew of was to pack it there in a bucket.

This sort of upset the trial and the Last Chance won.

Montana

MY DAD HAD A water right there.
He and Winters owned the creek.
Then the flume company started a flume,

and they used to steal the water all the time.
Winters was back East all the time
      so it was up to my father to keep the water going.
He used to have a lot of trouble.

He went up one time
      when the company had a big Dane watching the water.
He had turned the water into the flume
      and my father spoke to him about it.
The Dane said, "None of your Bismarck here."
My father was left handed,
      and the Dane started to hit my father
            over the head
                  with a shovel.
Father reached out with his left hand
      and grabbed him,
            and darn near drowned him.
A short time afterwards,
      they had trouble again.
Father went up there
      and they had another fellow there,
      but he improved on it;
            he pulled a gun on Father.
Father knocked it out of his hand
      and he had a big scar where the bullet went through.
When Father got through with him,
      he darn near killed him.
Nevada

———— ❧ ————

AROUND SMOKE Creek,
      Winters had big holdings,
            cattle ranges and sheep range
                  with springs that he didn't own.
Winters was afraid maybe someone would come
      and build a cabin or something,
            or come in with a small bunch of sheep,
                  or try to come in.

Here and there they would find a fellow
    who had started a place like that
        killed.
Winters had two henchmen out there.
    They did the work for him.
Jim Looper was more of a man than Walt Nealy.
    He couldn't stand it afterwards.
He got so he couldn't stand it,
    couldn't sleep or anything.
So one night he said, "By golly, I'll sleep tonight."
    Then he finished himself.

Nevada

———— ❧ ————

IT WAS A GOOD year
    and the wheat and oats crop in the county
        was above normal
    so those who had planted their land to grain
        reaped a good harvest.
Now the next thing, of course,
    was to haul their grain to market,
and so one of them filled a wagon box
    with about a hundred bushel of oats
    and started to Miles City,
        driving a several-horse team.
Before he had gone very far
    rain started to fall
    and the road became slippery and muddy
    and the farther he drove,
        the deeper and deeper the wagonload of oats
            began to sink into the mud.
Night came and he had to camp,
    and there was nothing to feed his horses except oats,
        so oats he fed them.
It continued to rain the next day,
    and he had to feed more oats to his horses.
Eight days later he arrived at the elevator in Miles City,

drove up on the platform,
and threw off a hundred-pound sack of oats.
That was all that was left
of his hundred-odd bushel he left Jordan with.
Worse yet,
he had to buy hay for his horses for the return trip!

Montana

ONE NIGHT MY DAD heard some people
crying for help
and there was a real blizzard going.
He got up,
and he lit his lantern,
and he could hear them crying
"Help! Help!
Isn't there somebody that can help?"
He went out and raised his lantern.
Then he took his team of oxen,
they were the best oxen that were ever born,
that ever lived.
He took that team of oxen and his lantern
up to where this sound was coming from.
It was a man and two daughters.
They had got tipped off the road
coming through there—
they had a no-good highway up there then—
because they had no lights to see in this blizzard.
They were just feeling their way along
and their horse got off the road.
Father helped him to get his wagon up.
Then they got his team and these girls
down to his cabin.
There was nowhere that they could lay down,
but they put the girls in the back
where they could keep warm.
They kept the fire going all night.

The next morning when it become daylight,
        the storm had subsided
and they decided to go see
        if they couldn't get that wagon straightened up.
They went up, fixed the wagon, got it ready
        and got the team on it.
The man said,
        "I don't have any money, brother, to pay you
                and I don't know how to pay you.
But I've got some alfalfa seed."
He said,
        "If you'll take some of that, I'll be happy."
Father said,
        "That's good enough for me."
So he took a sack
        and he gave him a big double handful
                of those alfalfa seeds.
So Father planted it
        and next year it multiplied
        and they got more seed.
That's where they got their first alfalfa seed.

Utah

———— ❧ ————

PEOPLE LIVED PRETTY far apart
        so they used to leave their homes open,
                with wood for a fire and food to eat,
        in case a traveler should stop by
                and be cold and tired and need something to eat.
Now, east of Monticello, there were two cattle companies,
        one in Dry Valley and the other up on the Mesa.
One morning, the Mesa cowboys
        got up and made an enormous pot of stew
                before they left
        so it would be ready when they got home in the evening.
While they were gone,
        the Dry Valley Company stopped there

on their way home from Colorado.
They helped themselves to the stew,
    finished the entire pot, washed all the dishes
        except one plate and one fork,
    and left for their home range.
When the Mesa cowboys got home,
    they found their stew gone
    and that one plate and fork there.
Wondered how big the man was
    who ate their entire tub of stew in one sitting.

Utah

IT WAS ABOUT FOUR or five miles
    right over the top of the mountain
        from our place to Cowles's ranch.
A man by the name of Nick Curnow was there by himself.
His horse threw him and stepped on his side,
    and broke his ribs away from his breast bone.
So he walked over the mountain to our place.
And I can remember us kids going out there,
    and he was leaning against a fence post.
I said, "What's the matter, Nick?"
He said, "I'm hurt!
    Tell your mother!"
So we went yelling in to Mother,
    "Somebody's hurt. Mr. Curnow's hurt!"
She got him into the house,
    said, "Go get your father."
Dad was a couple of miles away.
So we were as important as could be.
    We were saving the nation.
We ran all the way down there and yelled at Dad,
    "Mr. Curnow's hurt! Come quick!"
Well, people walked in those days,
    so Dad had to hike back and so did we,
        running along puffing behind him.
Poor Nick Curnow was too sick to move.

Dad says,
"I'm going into Gerlach and send for the doctor."
They had to wire to Winnemucca for Dr. Sweezy.
I heard my folks talking about it,
when they sent for a doctor in those days
he had to come whether he wanted to or not,
because he was the county doctor.
It wasn't a case of whether you wanted to;
he was sent for and that was it.
He came,
and Dad waited in Gerlach and brought him out.
I don't know what he did for Nick—
taped him up, I guess, somehow or other.
I guess he was tough,
because he lived a long time after that.
But that was life in the Far West, I can tell you that.
Nevada

———— ❦ ————

I SUPPOSE YOU HEARD about the big fire at Silver Lake
on Christmas Eve.
Well, they were having a program in the big room over the store,
and, of course, everybody came from miles around.
It was a big treat for the children.
Just as the program was ending,
someone stood up on one of the wooden benches
and knocked down an oil lamp
that was hanging overhead.
And the burning oil spilled out
and caught everything on fire.
Here were all these people
trying to get outside and down the stairs
and the people outside
were trying to get up the stairs to help.
And the stairs pulled away from the building.

There was a cowboy
downstairs in the store.

And when he saw what was happening,
    he jumped on his horse and rode for the doctor.
Well, that was Dr. Daly in Lakeview—a hundred miles away—
    and snow on the ground, pretty deep some places,
        and pretty cold weather.

Some people will tell you
    that he rode the same horse all the way.
        But of course he didn't.
He'd stop at the ranches along the way,
    tell them what happened,
        get a fresh horse,
            and away he'd go.
Got down to Lakeview and found the doctor.
He hitched up his buggy and headed back,
    changed teams at the ranches on the way back up,
        and got back to Silver Lake
            on the morning after Christmas,
    took care of all those people.

Oregon

A FAMILY WITH A ranch near Pilot Hill
    decided to have a barn dance.
The area was only sparsely settled in those days
    and no formal invitations were sent out.
Instead the word spread by word of mouth
    and everyone was welcome.
Dances were common in those days
    but there was always the problem
        of giving people directions
            as to how to get to the ranch.
Anyway this family devised a way
    of guiding people to the dance.
The ranch was near the highest peak in the vicinity
    so on the afternoon of the dance,
        they went up to the peak and lit a smudge fire
            as a signal of the location of the dance.

After sundown, they built a bonfire
    which gave people a pilot light to guide them.
Eventually the peak became known as Pilot Peak
    and the community was Pilot Hill.

California

THEY USED TO HAVE dances down there at the Grange Hall
    at Fort Rock
        about every month.
And, of course,
    everybody'd come from miles around,
    bring Grandma and Grandpa and all the kids,
        pile them in the wagon
            and come to the dance.
And everybody'd dance and have a great time.
    And when the kids got tired,
        why, they'd put them in the back room to sleep
            out of the way, you know.

Well, me and Charley Ivey used to play sometimes.
    I played the piano and he played the fiddle.
One time we got to fooling around
    and got to wondering what would happen
        if we mixed them kids up,
            put this one's shirt on that one, you know,
                and changed this one's blanket.
So that's what we did.

Well, these affairs would go on all night.
When it was time to leave,
    they just grabbed their kids and run.
The people would get home just at daylight
    in time to milk the cows.
The women would fix breakfast and go wake up the kids
    and they might have a kid from a couple up north
        of Christmas Lake, twenty miles away!
'Course, there was no communications in those days,

but a few old phones on a barbed wire fence.
Everyone had somebody's else kid.
It was quite an uproar.

Everyone accused us, but we said,
    "I was playing the piano
        and he was playing the fiddle,
           so we couldn't have done it
              because we were playing."
It took about a year before it started to get funny to them
    so then we told them.

Oregon

I WELL REMEMBER THE first baby that was born in the community
    and how the people gathered round the mother
        to get a glimpse of the baby
           the first time it was brought to church.
The family's name was Fletcher
    and it was the eldest little girl in this family
        who invited us all
           to our first Thanksgiving dinner.
When the folks came from miles around
    and came empty-handed,
        the mother couldn't help but wonder
           just what it was all about.
Suddenly it dawned on her that this was an "invitation affair"
    so she asked the little girl
        if she had invited the people there for dinner.
"Yes," she said.
    "I was lonesome."
She thought it would be nice to have a party.
So the women got busy and helped the mother
    prepare the dinner.
        And we had dinner,
    but certainly not anything like Thanksgiving dinner!

Colorado

Learning to Live with the Land

Mysteries

THE WEST IS A LAND unlike any other. It is a place where people cannot trust their eyes or ears, a place full of unfathomable holes, treacherous waters, unpredictable weather, elusive animals, strange half-human creatures. These stories are full of curiosity and puzzlement at a terrain that cannot be fully known and therefore can never be brought completely under human control.

WHEN YOU'RE OUT there on the desert,
 you hear it.
It's like a bell,
 rings regular, but far off.
Sometimes you hear it all night.
  It sounds like the bell on a burro.
   But it ain't nothing, nothing's there.

I once had a young feller for a partner.
The first time he heard it,
 he got up and made coffee
  for the outfit that he thought was coming.
 He wouldn't believe me
  when I told him it wasn't nothing.
He waited and waited
 and nobody came.
So the next morning he packed up and beat it.
California

THERE ARE A LOT of strange things out in that desert.
Ripley had an account once about the thundering mountain,
    and that was true.
There *was* rumbling out there.
    I heard it many a time.
It actually sounded, some days,
    just like the mountain was coming apart down inside.
One strange thing about it was
    that you could never get west of this sound.
No matter where you went,
    it always sounded like the thunder
        was coming from the mountain west of you.

I figure that it was probably blasting
    coming from the copper and silver mines
        out around Ely, Nevada,
    about a hundred miles west of there.
Those noises could probably travel underground.
Utah

ONCE WHEN I WAS coming back to camp,
    leading the horses along on a little trot,
there was a place for about a hundred yards or so
    that sounded like we were going over a hollow drum.
It just echoed back and forth down in there,
    and I was terrified before we finally got across it.
I guess this was partly because
    the fellow I was working with at the time
        had just told me about an experience
            that he and another fellow had
                along in there.

They had been riding up a wash not far from right there
    when one of the horse's hooves caved through the ground.
These guys thought that was a strange place for a badger hole,
    and the more they thought about it,
        the stranger it seemed.

So they went back
    and dropped a couple of rocks down in there,
        but they couldn't hear them hit bottom.
So they went back to camp
    and got a gunny sack and a can of kerosene,
and came back to the hole
    and soaked the sack in kerosene
    and lighted it afire
    and dropped it in the hole.
And that fellow swore up and down
    that that sack had burned out before it ever hit bottom.
I guess that's why I was so glad
    to get off that hollow ground.

Utah

———— ❧ ————

OUT AROUND THERE and up toward Eureka
    I was always terrified to go out at night
        because of the old prospect holes and other things
            that had been left.

I remember one fellow,
    part Indian,
was out one night.
He was walking around looking after his sheep
    and he fell into one of these prospect holes.
And it just happened that there was a log across the top,
    and as he fell
        he grabbed hold of that log.
So he hung on
    and tried to kick himself over and up the bank,
but he was quite a heavy fellow
    and the rocks would just crumble off
        and he couldn't get up.
        He just couldn't make it over,
            and it was just as dark as midnight
                down in the hole.

So he called and he yelled
        but the other sheepherder was sound asleep
                and he didn't hear him.
So this old guy finally wore himself right out.
He finally couldn't hold on any longer,
        so he just gave up and let go.
Well, he fell about six inches before he hit bottom.
Nevada

THERE ARE SUPPOSED to be bottomless pits
        on a ranch about six miles northeast of Flagstaff
                that date back to the days of the Apache raids.
When they were hard pressed,
        the Apache would drop from sight near Flagstaff
                and were later seen near Oak Creek Canyon.
This made people suspect
        that the bottomless pits
            were actually tunnels
                    that wound underground for many miles.
Arizona

MY GRANDMOTHER said
        that she used to hear all kind of Indian tales
                about Mount Knocti.
They said that it was a volcano,
        hollow inside.
Back before the white men came,
        Clear Lake used to rise and lower on its own,
                depending on the rainfall or lack of rainfall.
Where the lake came near the mountain,
        there was an opening.
From time to time, Indian braves
        would go into the opening on rafts
                and never come out.
My grandmother thought that maybe
        there was poison gases inside.

Once her two brothers were on Mount Knocti,
      digging for something,
            probably gold.
One of them dug into the ground
      and a hole opened up.
Not a big hole, but a hole nonetheless.
And the pick fell in
      and they never heard it hit bottom.
They were scared because of the possibility of poison gas
      so they ran away.
Later they could never find the place again.
California

WE TOOK A FAMILY vacation to Lake Tahoe the summer I was four-teen and I met a guy there who was about my age or a little older. The lake is really cold, you know. And this guy told me that when people drowned in the lake, their bodies froze and sank to the bottom where they couldn't be recovered. He made it sound as though the lake was full of these frozen bodies bouncing around on the bottom. I still think of that whenever I see the lake.
California

BEAR LAKE USED TO have a reputation
      for making people disappear.
In the winter,
      when the lake froze over,
            they used to take their wagons across the lake
                  to gather wood on the other side.
Every so often,
      a wagon would start across
            and never be heard of again.
When search parties went out,
      they would find no holes in the ice
            and never a trace of wagon or passengers.
Apparently the wind blew the snow around
      so there were never any tracks to follow.

Even now the lake is supposed to keep drowned bodies
        so that fewer are recovered
                than would be normal.

I heard that several people once took a dead sheep
        out into the center of the lake.
They tied it to a rope
        and dropped it into the lake the length of the rope.
And when they hauled the rope back up,
        the sheep was gone.

Utah

MY BROTHER AND I WERE out hunting for bear one year
        and we came across the set of tracks that we figured
                belonged to a grizzly,
                        they were so big.
So we tracked this bear all afternoon
        and the tracks finally led into this draw
                and then they disappeared.
Just disappeared!
        We covered every square foot of that draw,
                but with no luck.
So we just camped there overnight.
It was really spooky
        because we heard that monster bear
                howling and roaring all night.
The next day we came to this chimney type cliff
        and, lo and behold,
                there stood a monster grizzly some thirty feet up.
We spent that morning and afternoon
        circling that chimneyrock and couldn't find a way up,
                while that old bear kept growling
                        like the whole thing was some great joke.

Utah

THERE WAS ONLY two times in my life
    that I ever had a chance at a lion,
        and he outfoxed me both times.
One time I was going from Owl Canyon cross-country
    to Gray Mountain
        to the upper ranch there.
It was in the fall,
    along about twilight.
I come up over a ridge there on the top of that trail,
    and just before the trail dropped down in the meadows
        on the west side of Gray Mountain,
I looked across the draw,
    and there's a clump of spruce over there
        probably twice as big as a modern house.
And I seen that lion go in there.
Well, he couldn't get out of there
    and I thought,
        "This time I'm going to get me a lion."
I had my old rifle
    and I loaded that old gun, you know,
        and I kept waiting and waiting.
It kept getting darker
    and pretty soon it got to where I wasn't going to be able
        to see them sights.
I got to sneaking around on him
and there was a deep gully,
    a washout,
        right down under them spruce
            that went right down under me,
    but I couldn't see down there
        for a bunch of brush.
Shucks, I'd set there an hour
    by his tracks, waiting for that lion
        and he never stopped.
He come right on down
    and went down that washout

and I bet he was a mile from there
        before I knowed he was ever gone.
Colorado

———— ❧ ————

ONE FRIEND OF MINE was telling me
        about the time when he was out after elk.
He spotted a big bull elk on the side of a ridge
        as it was moving slowly along.
Before he could shoot it,
        the bull saw him and jumped behind a large tree.
Jim sat down
        and waited for the bull
                to come from out of the shadow of the pine.
Well, he waited there several hours,
        but he finally got impatient
                and slowly walked over to the tree,
        and was shocked to see the tracks of the elk
                follow the shadow up over the hill.
And he figured out
        that that smart old bull crawled on his knees
                in the shadows
                        just to escape from him.
Utah

———— ❧ ————

ABOUT 1965
        two hunters were driving up Pine Mountain
                in Mendocino County
        when they saw this gigantic buck
                with four points on his horns.
It was the biggest deer either of them had ever seen
        on Pine Mountain.
They named him Granddad.

Every year since then
        the Oaks Hunting Club hunters have seen Granddad
                feeding in the hills.

He is never exactly in the same place
  and they are not even sure
    if he is the same deer every time.
He is always standing on a hill in the open,
    but he always has one thick piece of brush near him
      to hide behind.
He seems to see the hunters before they see him
  and doesn't seem to be afraid,
    just stares back at them.
When they raise their guns,
  he jumps behind the brush and disappears.
If they send the dogs after him,
    the dogs can't find his tracks
      and no one sees him running away.
It's like he vanishes,
  just becomes invisible.
When the hunters do shoot at him,
  they always miss.

California

THERE WERE SOME PEOPLE drying fish up the Nehalem River
  when they heard this noise in the bushes.
Well, it wasn't the wind
  and they didn't think an animal
    could make a racket like that.
So they jumped into their canoe and took off across the river.
Well, they forgot their little dog
  and they heard it barking and barking
    and then suddenly the barking stopped
      and they heard this terrible crash.

Well, one of them went back the next day
  and found most of the fish eaten,
    and the dog dead,
      and Wild Man tracks all over the place.

Another time a man was camping there with his wife,
    when Wild Man came into the camp
        and took the woman.
The man went outside and found the tracks.
    He got a weapon and started to follow.
When he caught up with Wild Man,
    he discovered that his wife was dead.
So he shot Wild Man with the arrows he had
    and finally killed him.
The Wild Man turned out to be pretty much like other men,
    only much larger,
        and covered with hair like an animal,
            and he carried a club.

Oregon

WE WERE COMING HOME from football practice
    and down the bend that used to be there
        before they put the lake in,
            the road branched off.
We were going past there
    and saw this thing going across the cornfield.
He looked like one of them cavemen,
    long hair, Cro-Magnon, you know,
        complete with fur clothes.
Well, I've lived here most of my life
    and spent a lot of time in the woods,
        hunting and messing around,
    but I could never find no tracks of him.
As kids we heard stories of the Wild Man
    but never saw him
        'til coming home from practice that evening.
The two people that was with me,
    one got killed in Vietnam
        and the other's down in Crescent City, California.

Oregon

THIS HAPPENED IN February of 1962. It was before dawn, and raining and a little foggy when the dogs started barking. My brother-in-law got up and walked outside and saw something looking over the fence down toward the dogs. It looked like a large bear. He came back in and woke me up and said, "Come out and I'll show you the biggest bear you'll ever see." So I got up and walked outside with him but we didn't see anything.

I went back in to get a flashlight and a gun and my brother-in-law went around to the other side of the house to look back toward the brush. Just then something stepped over a little two-foot fence we have out there and stepped right toward him. Well, he screamed and stepped back and when he fell, I thought whatever it was had him.

I run to the window while he was crawling in through the door and I could see a big hairy body by the window. It tried to come through the door. My wife and brother-in-law tried to shut it, but couldn't get it to close. Something was holding it about four inches open. My wife yelled at me, "Hurry up with the gun. It's coming in through the door!" I said, "Let it in and I'll get it."

But when they let the door go and I ran to the window to look out, I could see it standing just a step back from the door. Then it turned and headed toward the driveway, then it disappeared into the darkness.

While it was standing near the door, we could smell a terrible odor. We don't know what the thing was. We've never said that it was "Big Foot." We just don't know what it was.

California

———— ❧ ————

THERE WAS A construction site
    with a few thousand drums of diesel oil,
        each weighing about 400 pounds.
There were a few D-6 cats there too,
      big tractors with claws four or five feet long
        to rip up the ground.
They must have weighed about 1200 tons apiece.

Anyway,
    the crew came back one morning
            and a whole pile of drums had been scattered
                    all around
and the tractors had been thrown around all to hell.
And in the area there were big footprints,
        about size 24q.
They said it was Big Foot.
California

 # Dangers

IF THE PLACE IS IN some ways mysterious, it is also dangerous. The dangers come most often from natural forces—the weather for one thing, wild animals for another. In these stories people cope with weather that is both unpredictable and extreme—flash floods and blizzards, snow and cold. And they contend with wildlife—wildcats, bears, rattlesnakes—that threaten, frighten, attack, and sometimes kill.

AT PYRAMID Lake during the late 1800s or early 1900s
    a sight-seeing boat was making a tour around the lake
        when a storm came up.
When the storm was over,
    there was no trace of the people or the boat.
Even though they searched,
    to this day nothing has been found.

The legend about the lake
    is that there is a vast, bottomless place in it,
and that the people and the boat were sucked down into it.
That's why no trace was ever found
    of either the people or the boat.
Nevada

THERE'S A STORY about a man
    who was driving a herd of hogs
        across a shallow part of the Snake River.
It was shallow enough

and the bottom solid enough
      so that he and his hogs crossed the river
            with no trouble.
The next day, when he was coming back from town,
      after selling his hogs at the auction,
he started to cross the river in the very same place.
But the bottom had dropped completely out
      of that part of the river.
The man and his horse were drowned
      and their bodies were never found.

Idaho

———— ❧ ————

AT THE COLD SPRINGS Pond there is a whirlpool of quicksand that can catch an unexperienced horseman unaware. They say that a buggy and team sank while attempting to cross the pond. When the townspeople went over the area with long poles, they couldn't find a bottom to the quicksand. And they never found the buggy and horses that were lost there.

Utah

———— ❧ ————

IN NORTHEAST BOX Elder County, the stage coaches, Pony Express, and freight wagons used to stop at what was known as the Bigler Hotel. They say that once a stagecoach on its way there came around the steep decline of Hampton Crossing too fast and plunged into the Bear River. The whirlpool sucked the outfit down and nothing was ever seen of it again.

Utah

———— ❧ ————

ONE TIME WHILE I was working at Cedar Mesa,
      the boss and I started down to Mexican Hat from our camp
            where they were drilling for oil.
Just before we got to Mexican Hat,
      a terrible rainstorm hit us.
We were in a Dodge coupe.
      All the old cars then

had the hood with these openings on the side
for ventilation;
I think they called them louvers.
Just as we entered a little wash
it began raining so hard
that it came in through the louvers
and wet the ignition so the engine quit.
We were afraid that a big flash flood
would come down through the wash.
We had to get that car out of there somehow.

Well, after the rain stopped,
I managed to get the car started again.
I looked back and there was water
just pouring up on the back of the car.
This big flash flood had come down from up in the hills.
I couldn't get out on the driver's side
so I crawled over on the other side
and climbed out.
Mr. Spencer was with me,
and he and I got out on a little island
that was sticking up probably six inches
above the water.
When I looked back the car had started rolling
and things happened quicker than I can tell it.
The water was hitting the car from behind,
causing it to roll past the island
until the strong currents of the larger stream
hit it sideways and rolled it over.
That's the last that we saw of that car.

So there we were stranded out there
and no way to get back but wade.
We were looking for the most likely place to cross.
My boss was over on the shore
and we couldn't hear him, of course,
because the water was making so much noise.

He clasped his hands and shook them,
        trying to tell us to take hold of each other's hands
                before we started to cross,
                        to support each other against the stream.
So we clasped hands and started across
        where it looked to be the shallowest.
But it was too deep for me;
        my feet went right out from under me.
Mr. Spencer was a big heavy man;
        he had a lot of weight above the water line
                so he could keep his footing.
He got behind me and kept boosting me
        until I was on the shore.
After we both got out, Spencer told my boss
        that when he clasped his hands together,
                he thought he was telling us good-bye.
We really had a laugh.

Utah

———— ❧ ————

ONE TIME FATHER was taking a bunch of cattle in.
        This was in May.
They thought they might have a little storm,
        but they hadn't had any storm
                and it was terribly dry east of Fish Spring
                and the cattle were dry.
That night—the fifth of May—
        they had two feet of snow.
In the morning
        they had over thirty head dead on the bed ground.

Utah

———— ❧ ————

JOHNNY WAS TELLING me
        that he went into the goat business once.
And they had twenty-six-hundred head of goats.
He said it was April, as I recall.

They were shearing them in April,
        and just after they got 'em all sheared
                there came up a terrific ice storm.
And he said the next day
        they had six hundred head of goats
                instead of twenty-six hundred.
He just saddled up his horse and said,
        "Partner, you take the goats.
        I'm going."
And he never came back.

New Mexico

———— ❧ ————

MY SON WAS IN school in Silver City
        and he got the measles.
So I had to come down there and take him out of school
        and take him home to the ranch.
So late in April, I come into town on the stage
                and got him
                        and we started out the next morning.
But the night before, the Gila was awful high.
No bridges then, so we forded the river going in.
        It was awfully high.
The next morning there was a new driver.
        His name was Graham
                and that was about the second or third trip
                        he'd ever made over the road.
He didn't understand what that river was.
So when we got to the river, it was abooming.
I never saw anything like it.
        It was just coming down great big old trees and brush.
                I seen great big cottonwood trees
                        coming down that river.
A Mexican was in the front seat
        and Burt, my boy, and I was in the back seat.
And the doctor had warned me, he says,
        "Now don't you let this boy get wet or damp

because it will go awfully hard with him.
          So be sure he don't get wet."
Well, this driver, I told him,
          "Don't go in that river."
          I says, "We can't cross that river."
"Oh," he says, "We crossed it last night."
I says, "I know you did
          but there's lots of changes in that river
                    since last night.
          You don't know where the quicksand is;
                    nobody knows.
          And look at the trees and look at the brush,
                    the stuff that is coming down that river."
And I says, "If we get stuck in the river,
          we can't get out;
                    that's all there is to it.
          If there was any place else on earth
                    that I could take my boy,
                              I wouldn't cross that river."
"Well," he says,
          "you'll just have to camp here
          for I'm going to cross."
And I says, "Yes, and you're going to get stuck."

So, of course, we started.
And right in the middle of the river
          the thing happened that I told him would happen.
The doubletrees broke
          and he got scared and let loose of the harness
          so the horses pulled out and left us
          . in the middle of that river.
Well, Burt and I climbed up on the back seat—
          water was coming through that stage —
                    clumb up with our feet on the seat
                              because I wanted to keep him
                                        from getting wet.
And the driver commenced to throw things out,

and I said, "Now look here,
 don't you throw another thing out of this stage."
I said, "If you lighten this stage,
 you'll roll it down the river."

So there we sat,
 nobody in sight nor hearing.
Then Burt looked out the back and says,
 "Oh, Mama, I see two men acoming ahorseback."
I said, "Oh, God, don't they look good!"
So they rode up and seen the condition we was in.
 So they swam their horses up to the stage.
Burt got up behind one of them
 and stood up on that horse so he wouldn't get wet.
Then the next one took me out
 and then they came back
 and got the Mexican and the driver.
So we got out
 and then they roped the stage
 until they pulled it out of the water.
When we got on ground Burt was just sick,
 he was scared so bad.

New Mexico

———※———

THEY COULDN'T BUILD down in the flat, you know,
 on account of the creek would get up
 and those floods would come.
So they were all built on the side of the creek.
And I was living in a house on the side of the creek.

And that morning I had had two or three cords of wood
 hauled in
 and I had put out a washing
 and had it on the line
 and I was in the kitchen cooking,
 making a pie.
I remember I had the rolling pin in my hand

and I heard the shouts—
      that's all the warning you had, you know—
"Flood's coming down."
There hadn't a drop of rain fell in Mogollon,
    not a drop.
And I run out with this rolling pin in my hand.
They was shooting a warning
    and I looked out up the creek
    and there was a wall of water coming down on us,
      just as high as one of them cabinets.
And right in the middle of it was a team of horses and a wagon.
    They belonged to Old Man York.
      He was out selling things.
And there was chickens in there and everything.
Well, it just took his team and wagon.

And right in front of where I lived
    there was kind of a foot bridge across
      where you could go back and forth,
and that team of horses and wagon hung up there
    and drowned both those horses there
    in front of my cabin.

There was two or three people drowned that day.
    There was one old Mexican woman
      and a little boy.
She was on the safe side of the creek,
    if she'd have stayed there,
but her home was on the other side
    and she couldn't stand it.
So she took this little boy by the hand
    and tried to wade that creek
and they were both drowned.

Arizona

ONE DAY IN JANUARY the ferryman went into Missoula on business, leaving me in charge of the ferry. The next morning, just about daylight, a man came for me to take him and his outfit across. It was 32 degrees below that morning but we made the trip over without incident.

Coming back about the center of the river I got in an ice-jam as there were large cakes of ice floating down the river. I tried every trick that I could think of but could not go either way. Finally by using the mooring cable on the end of the boat I was able to launch a small boat, but just as I was getting into it a large chunk of ice hit the boat, throwing me into the water.

I managed to get hold of the side of the boat and yelled for help, but could not make anyone hear as they were not out yet that early in the morning. However, by ducking first to one side under the water then the other one, I was able to keep from freezing until I could climb into the boat.

Montana

———— ❧ ————

IN THE WINTERTIME, why, we would go skating or sleigh riding. Once a bunch of us young people were skating over by the stone quarry. Over there the lake didn't freeze over the same as it did on the south end, so the ice was clear as glass. You could skate over it and see the little ripples under it in the sand underneath about six or eight feet down.

Ern Irwin, he dropped in a hole. Just went right down. The ice seemed to be fairly solid all around him, but he dropped in this hole. Albert Weston, being a pal of Ern's, crawled out there on his hands and knees to help him. Ern grabs him and gives him a jerk, and they both get in the hole. So we had two men in that ice-cold water. But they was lucky enough that when Ern first went down, Albert hung onto the schoolteacher who was skating with them. If she had got in there with all those dresses and things that she had on and not being able to swim, they would have maybe had more trouble. Well, we finally formed a chain on the ice, one hanging onto the next, and got them out that way. But that was one thing that ended skating. That was a close call.

Utah

———— ❧ ————

WHEN WE WENT TO town in the winter
    we would have to walk to keep warm.
I can remember being cold most of the time on these trips,
    or else tired from walking
    or both.

But on one occasion
    I got so tired and cold that I almost gave up.
On this particular trip I happened to be alone.
    It was ten below, I guess,
        and about eight inches of snow.
The heavy load of snow on the road had slowed me down.
It must have been about eight or nine at night,
    it was bright moonlight, though.
We didn't have the warm clothing that we have nowadays
    and I had walked so much,
    and became so tired and cold
        that I just figured I couldn't make it home.
I remember thinking
    that I would just climb in the wagon box
    and lay down—it wouldn't take long to die.
But then I recall saying to myself,
    "I'm just too young to die."
Besides, it would be real tragic on my parents
    to have the team pull up at home
        with me stiff on the bottom of the wagon box!
So, somehow I just kept going.
I don't remember the year this happened
    but I was sixteen years old at the time.
Utah

———— ❧ ————

TALK ABOUT weather!
In February 1871 the snow was two feet
    deep all over the Bitterroot valley.
No one had any doubt about there being irrigation water
    that spring.

It turned cold, so cold that the thermometer froze up
        and nobody knows how cold it was.
Chaffins and Caves had cattle on the range
        and our parents told us boys
                we better ride along the river
                        and see that the cattle were all right.
The brush was thick and the grass tall
        so we knew the cattle was okay
                if they did not get into air holes.

When we went through Corvallis
        we was pretty cold
                so we stopped at a saloon to get warm.
None of us had ever drank whiskey
        but someone urged us to
                and we did
                and that made us all feel better
                and we took a little more
                and that made us feel still better.
Chaffin bought a bottle of whiskey to take along
        but treated the crowd before we started
                so there wasn't anything much left in the bottle.
When we reached the hitching post where our horses were tied,
        the cold air had cleared our heads.
It occurred to Chaffin
        what would happen at home
                if he turned up with a whiskey bottle
so he decided to get rid of it there and then.
        Gave it a swing over his head and let fly.
It crashed through the window on the opposite side of the street
        and the window simply crumbled—
                the glass flew in all directions
                        like a shower of hail.
We mounted our horses and was out of sight
        before the people indoors could recover from the shock.

We rode about and saw to it that the cattle was all right
        and then started for home.

When we reached Corvallis again
    we stopped in Buck's store to get warm
        and found the crowd being entertained
            with the story of how cold it was.
"So cold that the big glass window in the drugstore
    simply exploded, broke into fragments."
That was the coldest day ever experienced
    in the Bitterroot valley.

Montana

I WAS HERDING SHEEP out there. I was only seventeen and living alone because the other two hired hands were brothers and liked to camp together. I needed some sugar, so I decided to walk to their camp and borrow some. Their camp was straight south up a little rise, not too far from my camp, maybe two miles.

Well, while I was over there, a storm come up. I was worried about the sheep straying in the blizzard. We decided that the brothers would leave their light on in case I had to come back, and that I was to fire the shotgun when I got back to my camp, so they would know I had arrived.

I began walking toward my camp figuring that I could find it if I just walked in the general direction. But the snow started coming down so heavily, I couldn't see and I couldn't tell where the road was.

All of a sudden I realized I was lost and I began to wonder if I would make it back. I didn't dare stop for fear that I might fall asleep or lose my sense of direction. I looked to the east toward their camp but I couldn't see a light. Then the horrible thought came to me that perhaps they had turned out their light and gone to bed. The only thing I could do was continue to walk and pray a little now.

You can imagine my joy when I glimpsed a flicker of light through the blizzard. I kept walking in that direction and finally arrived at their camp, soaking wet and very cold. The next morning when I looked out to see a foot of snow on the ground, I counted my blessings.

Utah

I GREW UP IN the Idaho mountains
> where it snowed seven to eight months of the year.
One year a new mail carrier started to go out for the mail
> during a period when the town was snowed in.
The old men in the town thought
> that the snow was in the sliding stage
so they warned the young man not to go out.
But he was bound and determined and he said,
> "I'd rather be buried for six months
> > than stay here and not get the mail."

After he left, he wasn't heard from for six months.
Several times men went out with poles to hunt for him.
Finally, one day that spring,
> my brother and I were picking flowers on a hillside.
And we saw the men coming in with the poles
> and two men in the back were carrying a body
> > on a stretcher.
It was the mail carrier.

Idaho

THESE TWO FAMILIES, the Worleys and the Shumates, were homesteading pretty near each other at Pine Mountain. Once when Mr. Shumate went into Rock Springs for supplies, his wife decided to visit Mrs. Worley while he was gone. So she took her big white Persian cat and set off. But when she got to the Worleys, she discovered her friend had gone to Rock Springs too, so, after she rested for a bit, she started back.

Mr. Shumate stayed in Rock Springs for several days. He saw Mr. Worley on the street one day and asked about Mrs. Shumate, but Worley said he hadn't heard anything of her, that a bad blizzard had struck about half an hour after she left their place.

So they organized a search party, and they searched for a week, but they couldn't find a trace of her. After the first party gave up, a second one was formed. They left town early on a

Sunday morning and searched all over the country between the two homes, wading in snow up to their waists at times. When the party broke for lunch, three of them decided to keep looking. They figured how far Mrs. Shumate could be expected to have travelled before the blizzard struck and what direction she would probably have taken and about how long she might have endured the cold and wind. They decided to leave the rim and search through a bunch of timber. They had gone only a few hundred yards when they came upon her body lying face down in the drifted snow. Her cap had been pulled off by tree limbs and her glasses were broken. She had evidently become frightened, had run 'til she was exhausted, then fallen in the snow and was overcome by the cold.

They took her body to Rock Springs for burial.

There was no trace of the cat. Two years later two families from Rock Springs were in that district deer hunting in October and the children found a big blue-eyed white cat. It was terribly wild, but the children captured it and brought it back to Rock Springs. It was believed to be Mrs. Shumate's cat.

Wyoming

———— ❧ ————

OUT AT THE Thompsons' cabin several years ago,
    there was a woman staying there.
She was writing a novel.
Well, she was there in the winter.
    And there's no electricity or phone out there, of course.
And she got snowed in
    and must have got cabin fever,
because when they went out to check on her,
    they found that she had left the cabin and walked around
        before freezing to death.
And they found pages of her novel she was writing
    all scattered around in the snow.

Wyoming

———— ❧ ————

FRANK WALKER USED to deliver the mail here in the valley
    and on over the mountains into California.
He told me that one time
    when he was on skis
        packing in first-class mail,
he had a mountain lion follow him for quite a ways.
He said every time he stopped,
    the lion would stop.
He said he just stayed so far back of him.
But he said he was glad
    when he got in sight of Markleeville.
See, the lion dropped out of sight then
    when he come in sight of the town.

Nevada

I REMEMBER one time,
    Clint Palmer, who was my age,
    went with me and my father
        out on the mountain for the summer.
One day they made us stay in camp for some reason.
We stayed in camp that day
    and were playing outside around the wood pile,
        when we looked up
           and saw a mountain lion.
The lion was on the side of the hill
    and it wasn't trying to bother us,
        but I was never so scared in my life.
We went in the house
    and shut and barred the door
    and piled everything we could up in the windows.
That's how the men found us when they came back that night.

Utah

MY OLDER BROTHER Paul and I
    were hunting elk in the Little Greys in 1930.

We'd hunted for several days
        and had nothing to show for it.

One afternoon when we were on foot
        and several miles from camp,
                we had an argument about the quickest way back.
He wanted to follow the trail
        and I wanted to shortcut around the mountain.
So we split up.

The farther I got,
        the more I realized I was wrong.
The going got heavy
        and I began to hurry.
When I came to a steep little ravine,
        I just slid right down into it.
And got a surprise!
There was a big bull elk there, laying down.
        I landed right in front of him.

I didn't even have time to move—
        the elk was that much quicker than me.
He was on his feet in an instant
        and I was looking up into his face
                maybe five feet away.
He lowered his horns toward me
        and I could see the long hair on his neck
                falling toward me.
Then he thought better of it
        and bounded off over the bank.
And there I lay weak as a kitten.

Wyoming

⟨⟩

WHEN I WAS ABOUT sixteen years old
        my mother sent me up to the herd in the canyon
                to get a fresh lamb for our meat.
I had to leave in the evening

so it was dark most of the way.
My horse knew the way pretty well
but he was a bit skittish on the way up the canyon.
Finally, I reached the sheep camp cabin
and piled into bed with the rest of the boys
on the front porch.
In the morning we discovered
that a bear had gotten into the sheep
and killed several lambs.
It had dragged the lambs under the porch to eat on them—
right underneath where we were sleeping!

So I headed down the canyon
without the lamb I was sent for
because the bear had killed it.
As I traveled
I could see the tracks my horse had made
the night before
and over each track was the print of a bear paw.
That bear had followed me
the whole way up the canyon
the night before!
No wonder my horse was skittish.

Utah

———— ❦ ————

THE PEOPLE IN Tres Piedras liked to talk about a certain grizzly bear that appeared in the area in the mid-1930s, killing cattle. One rancher decided to go after the bear. He and his hands agreed to meet at a line camp high in the mountains near where the cattle were killed. But at the end of the day one man had failed to arrive.

When they went looking for him, they found his body at the bottom of a ravine. Some people believe that the cowboy simply fell to his death, but others say that the bear killed him.

Then, about two years later, people found a sheepherder's slashed body near his camp in the mountains near Tres Piedras.

He had apparently been watering his horses at a nearby stream when he was attacked. Certain people did not believe that the bear had done it. They said that the strain of living away from civilization had caused the sheepherder to commit suicide. But most people blamed the bear.

New Mexico

THERE WAS A COWBOY who worked at a ranch up north of here.
    I didn't know him,
        I've just heard about him.
It was a number of years ago that this happened.
Anyhow, he was a pretty popular young fella
    and people were shocked
        when he turned up dead one day,
           out on the range.
They couldn't figure out what had happened
    and the doctor was too far away to call
        so they went ahead and buried him.
Gave his clothes and saddle and boots to his cousin
    who was working there too.

Well, his cousin put the boots on
    and they fit him pretty good.
        But then he suddenly got sick and died too.
And the same thing happened to his best friend
    when he put the boots on.

When they looked at the boots,
    they found a pair of rattlesnake fangs in the heel.
A snake had bitten the first young cowboy
    and the fangs had broken off in the boot
        but they were still poisonous.
So when the others put the boots on,
    they got stuck with the fangs
        and got poisoned too.

Nevada

PART THREE

Measuring Up to the Place

The Story continues to evolve as the storytellers describe
how the land fosters particular qualities
in the people who live there,
how their characters are shaped
in the process of meeting its challenges,
how westerners ultimately
come to belong to the place.

Measuring Up to the Place

Qualities

T HE QUALITIES MOST ADMIRED by westerners, to judge from the stories they tell, are those that emerge in response to some challenge from the natural environment, from the place itself. Among those traits are an understanding of the land-scape that comes from long experience; resourcefulness, the ability to use one's wits to cope with the unexpected; fearlessness, even recklessness, in the face of danger; and toughness, that ineffable quality called "grit."

To save one's own life, or others', through any of these qualities—even to be willing to take one's own life in the face of an insurmountable challenge—is to behave like a westerner, to be a match for the place itself.

———

AROUND JACKSON Hole, Wyoming,
        they tell a story about the Gros Ventre slide
            where half a mountain slid.
A lot of the early settlers lived at the base of the mountain.
There was an old mountain man
        who roamed the hills
        and was sort of a lone wolf.
One day, on top of the mountain,
        he noticed a split in the earth.
When he checked it later, it had grown wider and deeper.
So he decided to warn the people in the valley
        that the mountain was going to slide
        and that they had better move.

92

No one believed him
    or paid any attention to him.
Sure enough, one day
    half the mountain slid into the valley
    and buried a lot of homes and people.
After the slide
    the old man disappeared
        and was never seen again.
Some people think he was buried in the slide.
    Others think he was some kind of prophet
        who just mysteriously disappeared
            after delivering his message.

Wyoming

———— ❧ ————

THE FIRST MORNING WE were at the ranch, I washed our clothes and hung them out. It was a beautiful day, not a cloud in the sky. Half an hour later, Melba Warren came into the house, her big, blue eyes flashing and those two blonde pigtails hanging behind her ears. She came up to me and said, "Get your clothes in the house, quick, 'cause it is gonna rain." I laughed and asked, "How do you know?" She replied, "'Cause I can smell it."

Before I could move, Melba jumped up and brought all my clothes in. As I stood there at the sink and tried to figure out what she was talking about, the sky broke loose and for five minutes the biggest downpour I ever saw broke loose. I was so stunned! I don't think I even moved.

About five minutes later I looked out. The rain had stopped and I thought the place was on fire. The steam just rose from the ground, and there weren't even any water puddles around. The sun was out, Melba Warren was back outside playing, and the conversation went "We had a little shower. Too bad it didn't last."

New Mexico

———— ❧ ————

ONCE IN A WHILE there was flash storms there.
For instance, there was a beautiful spring

in what they called Trail Canyon
about four to six foot across
and about eighteen inches or two foot deep.
Crystal clear water.
The woodchucks and squirrels
had kept the grass trimmed around there,
it was just like a lawn.

I unpacked my horses and fixed dinner for the herder.
That was Gus Edler, and he was an old hand.
Soon as we got dinner over with, he says,
"I want this camp moved
right up there in that bunch of quaking asp.
This is not a good place to camp right down here."
Well, I was upset.
I thought he was a fool to want to go up on that hill
where it was dry
and most the trees were dead.

But a few nights after,
there was a flash flood hit there,
and there was logs went down through there
must have been thirty foot long
just went like matchsticks.
That water was all of twelve, fifteen foot deep,
just a mass of mud and water and timber.
It would've wiped us out right down there.

Utah

———— ❧ ————

BILL MCCARDLE WAS one of the best-known characters
in that part of Nevada.
One of the stories they tell about him was about the time
that he was working one of his claims,
about four miles away from his cabin.
Some rock caved in on him, and it broke his leg.
Well, he was miles away from anyone
and had to get to his cabin by himself.

But he was determined to get home,
    so he used his pick as a crutch.
It took him several hours,
        and he was in quite a bit of pain, of course,
            but he made it.

Once he got there, he had to set his own leg.
And it was a couple of days
        before anyone happened to pass by.
Finally when the doctor examined Bill's leg,
        he said he couldn't have done a better job himself.

Nevada

PAUL WAS WORKING for a pipeline company,
        laying line, in 1929.
One day the flat bed trucks were racing
        and Paul's legs were hanging over the edge,
            and somehow one of his legs got crushed.
No one knew what to do
        so he took out his own knife
            and finished cutting it off.
Then he took his shirt off
        and made a tourniquet
            and they took him to the hospital.

New Mexico

"LONG GEORGE" FRANCIS was one of the characters in old Havre. The story they like to tell about him the most is about how he died.

He was accused of stealing a mare and was asked to turn himself in, but before he gave himself up he said he wanted to see his girlfriend again. So on Christmas Eve he drove off north of Havre with presents and a crate of apples. On the way he was caught in a blizzard, his car turned over, and he broke his leg. But he decided to try to get to his girl's house anyhow. So he splinted his leg with pieces of the apple crate, and started working his way through the snow.

But he didn't get very far before he realized that he wouldn't
be able to survive the storm with his injuries. And he didn't want
to die a slow death, so he cut his own throat.

Montana

MY GRANDFATHER HAD HEARD of a small bunch of cattle
      that had not been shipped in the fall
           because the owner had broken his leg.
He found the place and asked the owner
      if he had these cattle in,
           that he was interested in buying them.
The old man said he had the cattle,
      but that they had been turned out for the winter.
He thought, though, that his wife could find them.
Supposing that the man meant to send her horseback,
      my grandfather rode on to the next place,
           promising to come back that night.
He returned about nine that evening,
      by which time the temperature had dropped
           to around thirty below.
He found that the wife had not yet returned,
      and immediately became convinced
           that she had frozen to death.
But the old man was not worried.
      "She's a pretty good woman," he said.
About eleven that night, the old woman returned,
      on foot, with all twenty-five head of cattle,
She explained that she had not found the cattle
      till almost noon,
           and that they were mixed with range cattle.
By the time she had gotten them separated, still on foot,
      it was dark;
           then she drove them home.
She seemed to think little of the experience,
      but my grandfather was speechless.

Montana

MY GRANDMOTHER moved to Wyoming
    from somewhere back East.
She came out here to be a schoolteacher
    in one of these little country schools.

She was walking home one afternoon
    when a blizzard came up all of a sudden
        and she was hurrying to get home.
She came to this sheep camp
    and she thought about stopping there
        until the storm quit.
But then she thought it wouldn't be proper for her
    to be alone with the sheepherder in his camp.
So she went on.
But she didn't go very far before she realized
    that she could very easily get lost in the storm
        and never find her way home.
So she decided that what was proper
    wasn't as important as staying alive.
And she turned around and went back to the camp.

Wyoming

THIS IS A TRUE STORY I heard from my uncle.
He'd been on a hunting trip in Yosemite.
    In those days the camps were fairly elaborate,
    with canvas tents.
And when they put the tent stakes in,
    they used a sledge-hammer.

The story was that the handle had broken on the hammer.
So they took the hammer off the handle
    and they took a rope and hung the hammer
        from a branch of a tree so it wouldn't rust
            and wouldn't get lost on the ground.
Well, then a bear came into camp and on his travels around,
    he bumped his nose right up against the sledge-hammer.

And it swung a little bit and came back
    and tapped him on the nose.
That made the bear a little bit irritated,
    so he slapped it a bit.
And it went out a little bit further and hit him again—
    BANG,
        right smack on the nose again.
And the bear got real mad this time
    and he took a real heavy swipe at it with his paw
        and the hammer went all the way up,
            over the branch and hit him
                right on the back of the head
                    and knocked him silly.
My uncle said all he saw
    was the bear's heels running back down the hill.
California

I DECIDED TO DRIVE up to Indian Creek Reservoir
    to camp for the night.
        Maybe do a little fishing.
So I drove about five miles up the canyon,
    decided to make camp in a thick grove of trees
        next to the lake.
There was nobody around there, had it all to myself.

After supper I decided to make my bed on the ground,
    then I decided, well, I better put it inside the Scout.
I had to leave the end gate down to make room enough.
I put my food up on top of the car
    so the chipmunks wouldn't get at it.

A real dark night, pitch dark, not a soul around.
    I went to bed.

About midnight the old Scout started rocking.
    I thought it must be a cow or something
        rubbing against it.

I got the flashlight, looked out the side window.
  And it looked like a cow or something
    walking around the side of the Scout.

About that time right at the end of my bed
  there was a big old brown bear
    looking me right in the eye.
Flashed my light in his eyes;
  about scared me to death,
    never seen any bears up in that country.

I didn't know what to do.
I knew that if he decided to come in there with me,
  I was gonna make a new opening
    in the other end of the Scout.
So I started hollering,
  his old red eyes just glowing at me,
    but he wouldn't move.
Stood right at the end of the bed,
  and he acted like he wanted to come in with me.
I hollered and kept my light on him,
  but he stuck around, didn't want to move.
After five minutes he finally decided
  to amble on down the country aways.
Boy, I was glad to see him go.
  I was pretty scared.
Jumped out, grabbed an old axe I had there
  and put it inside my bed
    in case he decided to come back.
Didn't have sense enough to close up the end of the Scout.

Anyway I finally got back to sleep
  and had quite a nightmare.
When I woke up, looked there at the end of my bed
  and that old bear was back,
    looked me right in the eye.

I didn't know what to do.

I grabbed my axe
      and started hammering on the old bed of the truck
        and hollering.
He just stood there eying me up,
      wasn't going to move.
I made quite a racket hammering on that old tin bed.
Finally he decided to move on.

The rest of the night I'd keep jumping up in the night
      and looking out there
        and I could see all these big black stumps.
They all looked like bear.
I didn't get any sleep the rest of the night.
About the time it started getting light,
      I got up and got out of there.
That was the only bear I ever saw up in that country.
He wasn't supposed to be there,
      but he was.

Utah

OLD BILL BURRIS, up in the Judith Basin,
      told about an old black bear
        with an overgrown taste for horse flesh.
By the time he'd slapped down
      some twenty-five or thirty young colts,
        he'd made himself pretty unwelcome,
and everybody that could squint down a pair of gun sights
      and squeeze a trigger
        was out gunning for him.
But it wasn't doing any good,
      so Bill and his brother,
        along with some twenty-five other cowpokes
          decided to gang up on the bear.

They all made an agreement not to shoot at anything
      but that bear,
        so that when shots were heard,

they were all to make for that spot,
              just in case help was needed.
Well, they had been combing the hills for two days
        and were working some of the foothills
              near the English Sapphire Mines.
Bill and another fellow was riding together
        when they hear shots.
They know that some one of the boys is in a tight spot
        so they lit out hell bent for leather.
They top a low rise and in a little clearing
        they see a man skinning up a big bull pine.
They can't see what is going on at the foot of the tree,
        so they leave the horses and approach on foot.
They don't break cover until they're within
        about twenty-five yards of the big pine.
And there they see Bill's brother backing out on a big limb,
        and following him out on the very same limb
              is the biggest black bear they have ever seen.

Bill's brother is desperately hanging on with one hand,
        and motioning frantically to the bear with the other,
              hollering, "Go back, GO BACK, you damn fool,
                    or we'll both fall off!"

Montana

———— ⚘ ————

WELL, OLD MAN Zuk was a man that he wouldn't work.
        You couldn't get him to work.
        He said they could hang him but he wouldn't work.
Anyway, he was hunting.
        He'd hunt and kill meat,
              but he wouldn't work.
So he thought he had killed this bear,
        so he put his gun down by the side of a tree
              and went to go to this bear.
You know they always cut their throat to let them bleed
        when they kill 'em,

and he went to go to this bear,
    but the bear was only stunned
        and so him and the bear had a fight.
And he didn't have any gun, of course.
And they said the only thing that old man Zuk had on
    when he got through with the bear
        was a shoe.
He was just scratched and tore all to pieces,
    but he finally got the best of the bear.

New Mexico

THIS NEIGHBOR of ours,
    once when he was out in the woods,
        he came across this old mother bear.
And all he had to fight with was a pocket knife.
    He'd managed to get it out of his pocket,
        but the old bear slapped it
            ten feet away from him,
                slapped that knife out of his hand.
Well, then he had nothing to fight with.
But he managed to get down and get a rock;
    he was a big strong man
        and he beat this old mother bear off.

But he always said that the reason the bear attacked him
    was because he had this little black pup in his arms
        and the pup was probably whining
            and she thought it was one of her cubs,
                probably.

Well, when he got down in sight of where we lived,
    my brother and another fellow always had guards out
        because they were watching for Indians.

Well, when he got in sight of the house,
    my brother and this fellow that was with him,
        named Tom Coffee,
    saw him,

and he wobbled and staggered around
    so they didn't know what to make of it,
and my father says,
    "Just watch that man"—
        he'd wave his hat once in a while, you know,—
    "it may be Indians that he is signaling to."
So he came on a little farther and fell
    and as he fell he waved his hand or his hat
        and the boys saw him
so they went to him
    and this bear had just clawed him,
        just scratched him all to pieces;
            he couldn't come any further for loss of blood.
And they brought him down to our house.

So this fellow, Tom Coffee,
    he didn't know anything about surgery or anything,
but something had to be done with this man
    because he was losing so much blood.
So mother sat down and ripped up one of her dresses
    that was sewed with silk thread
and he took that thread
    and sewed this man's wounds up.
And that fellow lived.
If he hadn't been such a big strong man,
    he never could have whipped that bear with a rock.

New Mexico

———

WHEN I LIVED in Montana,
    I met an old man who told me a true story
        that happened to a friend of his.
He and a bunch of ranch hands were out rounding up cattle
    one day in the fall.
When night came,
    one of the men didn't come back.
Well, they couldn't go out to look for him
    because they knew there were grizzly bears around.

And they were in the woods where it was dark
    and they couldn't see anything anyway.
Well, they found out the next morning
      that as the man was on his way back to the camp,
         he came across a grizzly bear,
            so the man played dead.
That's the only thing you can do with grizzly bears.

Well, the bear stayed with him all night.
      He'd walk away and sit down for awhile,
         then come back and chew on him a little
           or maul him with his claw.
Finally, toward morning, the bear left him
    and the man was able to crawl back to camp.
Now this man had short cropped hair
    and when he got back to camp
        his hair had turned completely white.

Montana

THIS IS A true story.
My grandfather had a huge big hand like so
    and he was a raw-boned, strong man.
Well, the dogs had something treed
    up this little gulch right out here.
He thought it was a coon up the tree
    and he took a shotgun
      and he went out there.
The tree came right up out of the bottom of the gulch,
    and about even with him
      he could see this panther
        against the side of the tree.
So he shot him with the shotgun.

Well, it broke the panther's back
    and the panther fell down amongst the dogs,
But he could still use his front paws and his teeth
    and he was just knocking the spots off the dogs.

So my grandfather took a match
       and he lit the grass afire along the edge of the bank
            and was peering down to try to see
                 what was going on down there
and the bank gave way
       and down there he went.
And when he hit bottom,
       his hand closed over this rock
            about the right size
And he took it
       and he conked the panther over the head with it
            and killed him.
That panther cut up some of those dogs pretty badly
       and they had to sew them up, you know.
But that happened right out here
       within a couple of hundred yards of this house.

California

A WILDCAT GOT INTO our potato cellar one time
       and Mom wanted someone to get rid of it
            so she could go in safely for potatoes.

So Fletcher,
       who we never could decide was fearless or brainless,
            volunteered for the job.
Dad said,
       "We'll hold the cellar door open for you, Fletcher,
            so you can see what you're doing."
Fletcher said,
       "No, give me a pitchfork and shut the door.
            I want to give the son-of-a-bitch a fair chance."

Idaho

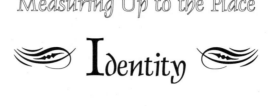

Measuring Up to the Place

Identity

Having learned to live with the land, having had their characters formed by it, the storytellers know how to distinguish themselves from easterners, newcomers, dudes, and other species of outsiders. In these stories that proclaim western identity, outsiders most often reveal their status by their ignorance or misunderstanding of some feature of the natural environment. And this is perhaps the most appropriate way in which the distinction between insiders and outsiders should be made, for it is the natural environment of the West that has been the most powerful force in shaping those who live there.

The Story began with a journey and ends with the intimation that outsiders in these stories may be on their way to becoming westerners themselves.

AROUND THE CORNER from the Santa Fe Sears store, there was a small restaurant where I sometimes had lunch.

The woman seated next to me ordered posole. When it was served, it looked like a harmless bowl of soup, so I ordered the same. One spoonful made me think I had swallowed a live coal. I looked at the woman beside me. She was eating with evident enjoyment—with tears rolling down her cheeks!

I had to pay for two bowls of soup because I pushed aside the bowl of fire and ordered vegetable soup, better suited to my eastern palate.

New Mexico

WE WERE RIDING along looking at calves.
I had some hay in the pickup
        for some of the more remote critters.
We came to a cross-fence gate
        and I asked the dude
                if he knew how to handle that kind of gate.
He said "Sure" and hopped out of the truck.
He opened the gate easy and I drove through,
        stopped and waited.
When he didn't get back in the truck right away,
        I looked back.
He had closed the gate all right
        but was on the other side of the fence.
I watched him try to climb back over
        and catch his slacks on the barbed wire.
Finally he reopened the gate
        and walked through
                and closed it.
This time he stayed on the right side of the fence.
He looked at me kind of funny, but I just smiled.

Oregon

A DUDE WOMAN at one of the local ranches
        decided to go riding alone one afternoon.
The wrangler told her that if she became lost,
        to give her horse his head
                and he would come home.

As usually happens, the woman did become lost,
        but fortunately for her
                she was not too far from the ranch.
She remembered the wrangler had told her
        to let the horse have his head,
so she proceeded to take off her saddle and bridle
        and send the horse on his way.
The wrangler knew the country

and noticed the direction the horse came from.
He finally found the woman
    waiting patiently by her saddle.

Arizona

———— ❧ ————

THEY TELL A LOT of stories about dudes in Arizona. Like the one about the easterner who stopped at a trading post near Winslow, walked into the store, up to the trader and asked, "What color uniforms do the cattle guards wear?"

Arizona

———— ❧ ————

I WAS TAKING A TOUR bus through Yellowstone one summer. And there was a big crowd that had gathered at one spot to watch a herd of elk feeding. An old lady on my bus who was from Newark, New Jersey, watched the elk for a while, and then she asked me, "When do deer turn into elk?"

Wyoming

———— ❧ ————

MY COUSIN FROM Pennsylvania came to visit one summer
    and we were driving out west of Laramie.
She looked around at all that sagebrush and said,
    "Well, it'll be real nice
        when all these little trees grow up."

Wyoming

———— ❧ ————

THESE HUNTERS WERE out hunting
    and they were, I guess,
        forty miles from the nearest town.
And this gentleman decided he needed some castor oil
    very, very badly.
He was really sick and needed a physic.
But it was forty miles to the town where he could get any.
So anyway they made the trek—
    I don't know if they were on horseback or walking.

So he went into town to get his castor.
So when he told the druggist what he wanted,
    he got the biggest laugh!
Because there was Indians there, you know.
And they laughed and they laughed and they laughed
    because it happened that the hunters were camped
        in a grove of cascara trees.
Now cascara is an old-fashioned remedy, a laxative.
In fact the oldtimers, they'd cut some of the bark
    and soak it in water and then drink it.
So they laughed and laughed and laughed
    because these fellows were camped in a cascara grove.
All he'd had to do was get a little bark off the trees for his physic.
California

———— ✿ ————

THERE'S THE STORY IN Mountain Home about the two airmen who
went elk hunting for the first time in their lives. It seems that they
came proudly up to the warden, eager to show off their prize.
There in the back of the pickup, poorly skinned and very poorly
cleaned, lay a large animal, with an elk tag properly attached.
There was only one slight problem. The animal in question was
not an elk, not even a deer, but a mule!

At this point, the story has several variants. One version says
that the poor mule even still had its shoes on.

As to what happened, there are again variants. According to
one story, the warden was laughing so hard, the airmen knew
something was wrong. Finally, the warden choked out something about a mule, whereupon one airman asked, "You mean
it's a mule deer?"

Idaho

———— ✿ ————

THERE WAS A UTAH hunter who took his California friend
    out to deer hunt for the first time.
The Utah hunter said,
    "You go this way around the mountain

and I'll go the other way.
If you get anything, send up a flare
and I'll do the same.
But he warned his friend,
"If you do get something, go claim it quick,
'cause some of these hunters'll try
to steal your deer!"
Well, they set out
and just before they were to meet
on the other side of the mountain,
the Utahn heard some shots
and pretty soon he saw a flare go up.
"By golly, he's got one," he said
and started running in the direction of his buddy.
Just before he got there,
he heard someone arguing and thought,
"Oh, no, someone's trying to steal
my buddy's deer."
When he came to the clearing
he saw his buddy and another man
standing over the dead animal.
He heard the other man exclaim,
"Okay, okay, you can have your deer,
just let me get my saddle off him!"
Utah

DOWN IN THE DRIFTS of the mines, they had what they called a grizzly. That was some iron rails put together about three inches apart, that they let the ore go through, so they could break up the larger pieces.

One of the workers there told a new man, he says, "Be careful, there's grizzlies when you go out." This kid says, "My gad, if there's any grizzly bears out there, I'm not going!"
Utah

SEVERAL YEARS AGO when the El Escalante Hotel in Cedar City was the headquarters for the railroad people, all the people coming from the East and different places to see the national parks would stop there at this hotel. Brose Thompson was one of the old residents of Cedar City and a great fellow to tell stories. So he was sitting there talking to one of his friends one night and here come a bunch of rich folks from New York. They'd come in on the train and they were staying at the hotel, and they were going to go by bus to the parks the next morning.

So Brose started talking to his friend and he kept talking a little louder and a little louder and finally he got an audience to listening. And he says to his friend, "You know, if the government wants me to paint Bryce Canyon next year, I'm gonna turn down the contract." He says, "If they think I'm gonna hang by ropes and paint that canyon with spray guns at the price they pay, they're crazy!"

Utah

———⚘———

ONCE WE MOVED into town
      it seemed everyone wanted to become acquainted with me.
I was still not familiar with their speech and ways.
The men would stand around and talk by the hour.
As I look back, I realize
      they were just making conversation to hear me talk.
            I was the stranger.
Yet I wasn't smart enough to figure it out then.

One day I walked into the gas station
      and two men were talking.
A third man came in and the two greeted him with
      "Hello Fizzer."
This Fizzer turned to them and said,
      "Been looking all over for you.
      I want you to go down behind El Paso Number Two
            and bury those two dead men."
They calmly said, "Okay. Get it this evening."

I turned on my heels, went home,
    and got out my suitcases and started to pack.
My husband came into the apartment and says,
    "What are you doing?"
I answered, "I'm going home.
    People out here can't even give a dead man a decent burial."
It took a lot of talking before I would believe
    the men had been talking about two pieces of pipe.
Later Fizzer Phillip became a dear friend
    and he used to always bring this up.

New Mexico

I DO REMEMBER ONE time some inspector came up. Now, I suppose he was a government inspector, I don't know what. He seemed like a young man to us, so he couldn't have been very old, because most grown-up people seemed like they were quite old.

He had a new pair of boots, high boots clean up to his knees practically, that laced up. Of course, us kids were intrigued with them because the men around there didn't wear those kind of things.

Well, poor guy, these were brand new boots. So Dad showed him everything that he wanted to see—right up over the top of the hill, the hardest way to go. "Over here's another claim" says Dad. "No! I think I've seen enough" says the inspector. His feet were killing him, the poor guy.

Nevada

I HAD A KIND OF AN amusing experience with a forest ranger once.
I worked for the Forest Service one summer
    with Ozro Hunt and Marion Hunt and Harold Butt,
        building trails and fences.
We three got along well,
    but while we were at Kigalia one time,
        a new forest ranger came and camped with us.
He was just out of school,

had never been out on the range,
and he was just as green as he could be.
He was going to Monticello the next day;
it was quite a ways over there
and he didn't know the trail
and he was asking about it.
Marion Hunt says,
"Now don't you worry one minute.
That old horse knows that trail.
You go to sleep and get a good night's rest
and we will call you early in the morning
and put you on the trail early
and that old horse will never turn from that trail
until he gets to Monticello."

So the fellow finally quieted down and went to bed
and was asleep within five minutes
after he hit the pillow.
As soon as he was sound asleep,
Marion said,
"Oz, you go out and get his horse
and I will fix breakfast for him."
So Oz went out and brought in the horse and mule,
saddled the horse and fed it a little grain,
while Marion cooked breakfast.
And along about eleven that night,
Marion went over and shook him
and said, "What is the matter with you?
You going to sleep all day?
I thought you wanted to get an early start!"
The fellow groaned and said, "It's not morning yet."
But Marion routed him out of there.
He said, "I am not hungry yet."
Marion said, "You eat your breakfast
and we will throw your pack on the mule while you eat."
So he got his breakfast and they went out,
packed up his mule, took him out and put him on his horse,

took him over about a half a mile
and got him out of the pasture,
and put him on the trail.
They said,
"Now you just let this horse follow the trail."
Then they came back in and went to bed.

That fellow rode all night.
That old horse didn't leave the trail all night;
he just plugged along
and by daylight the next morning,
the ranger was on top of the Blue Mountains,
looking down at Monticello.

Those Hunt boys were great jokers.

Utah

———— ❧ ————

THERE WAS THIS sheepherder had one leg. How he got one leg, I don't know, but he had just a wood stump on one leg. Of course, he could ride a horse and nobody knew any different. And cars still were a novelty in southern Utah then—I don't know what year that would've been, but they were a long ways behind the rest of the country.

But some folks with New York license plates were traveling up on Cedar Mound and this old sheepherder saw this car down there. And it was such a novelty, he went down to take a look at it, you know, to see what it was about.

Well, in the course of the conversation, he told them he was the roughest, meanest critter on the whole mountain. And they said, "What do you mean?" And he said, "Why, I got this butcher knife" and he pulled this great big old fishing knife out—a twelve-inch long blade. He said, "I got this butcher knife and I can jab it RIGHT in my leg, and I won't even yell." They said, "Aw, you can't do that." And he said, "You wanna bet?" They made a wager on the deal. Old Pete pulled out his leg and just pegged the knife up in it—DINNNNG! And the blade was

wobbling back and forth. The New Yorkers leaped in their car
and took out. Never to return.

Utah

———— ❦ ————

HUGH ROWNDY WAS a character in Escalante
     in the early part of this century.
The town always looked a little run down,
     with paint scaling off and weeds in the yards—
          people don't have water for lawns.
So Hugh Rowndy and two other men
     were sitting up against a main street store front,
          whittling,
               when a tourist came passing through.
He looked around and saw how run down everything was.
And since he'd just come through
     the beautiful canyon into Escalante,
          he got very disgusted with the place.
So he saw these three loafers sitting against the wall,
     whittling,
and he walked up to them and said,
     "What's the matter with you people?
          Don't you have anything else to do?"
And Hugh Rowndy spoke up and said,
     "Mister, we don't even have to do this
          if we don't want to."

Utah

———— ❦ ————

SELDOM SEEN SLIM WAS a prospector in the Panamint Valley, and
he used to love to fool the tourists. Once he gathered up all the
fool's gold he could find and stationed himself and his burro
alongside the main road that runs through the valley. When he
heard a car coming, he took his pick and shovel and began chipping away at some rocks.

    Well, the car stopped and the tourists poured out, real excit-
ed to see a real live prospector. Slim pretended to ignore them

and kept on chipping and digging. One of the tourists thought he would make a joke and asked him what he was doing—digging roots? Slim just gave him a glance and kept on with his digging.

Then the others started asking him about what he was doing, and he finally admitted that he had found a trace of gold here. They were skeptical and laughed, so Slim condescendingly tossed a piece of fool's gold to them. Obviously they didn't know the difference between fool's gold and real gold and they asked if they could buy it for a souvenir. Slim gave it some long, hard thought, then named an exorbitant price, which they paid. Then they piled back in their car, delighted to have a wonderful story to tell their friends and, as proof of the story, a piece of gold.

California

FOUR YOUNG KIDS came to work in the mine.
They'd heard of some rich ore there
    and they wanted to get some good specimens.
Vic Littlefield was running the tram.
He told the four kids
    that he'd try to get them some good specimens
        out of the mine.
So when he was in there,
    he picked up a bunch of pretty good-looking rocks
        that was loaded with pyrites—fool's gold.
He figured that'd satisfy them.
He came out and gave the kids these specimens
    and, boy, they was all hopped up;
        they thought they really had something.
There was an old man there,
    he knew a little bit about ore
        but the kids, they didn't know anything.
So these kids started handing the specimens to the old man
    to see which one had the best
        and what he thought of them.
The old man, he looked them over pretty good
    and pretty soon the samples got all mixed up.

And the kids, they began arguing about
    which sample belonged to which one
        and they got pretty mad about it.
They darned near came to blows.
Finally, the old man that was looking them over, he says,
    "Well, I don't know about gold," he says,
    "but I never did see anybody foolish enough
        to give it away."
That kinda straightened the kids out.
    I guess they didn't figure they had much.

Utah

———— ❧ ————

THIS FELLOW FROM New York had bought property in Grand Lake and paid for it with hard cash and built his house and garage and one thing and another, and then he went back to New York for the winter. This fellow's property was right where the road comes around into Grand Lake where they ask the tourists to stop and look at the lake. That was a beautiful view of the lake and this being a tourist town that was one of the attractions.

Well, when this fellow bought this property, he put his garage up right there where it blocked the view. So the citizens of Grand Lake went to him and asked him to put his garage somewhere else. But he was a know-it-all and he wouldn't do it. So it was a thorn in the side of the Grand Lake people.

Now all the tourists are gone in the wintertime and when clean-up day came—I think about the first of May—in Grand Lake they were all busy cleaning up their yards and somebody said, "Why don't we go and take down that garage that blocks the view?" So the road commissioner said, "Well, if you want to do that I've got some dynamite to blow the rocks off the road. And the superintendent of schools and the postmaster and the mayor all said, "We'd better not send just a few people up to do that; it's better that the whole town go."

So the entire town went and those who didn't want to go were told to go along anyway. The county commissioner, the county superintendent of schools, the mayor of the town, the postmaster, the town council, all the people of Grand Lake went up and planted the dynamite under the garage and blew her sky high. I was the D. A. then and the New York man came into my office and said, "Do you allow people to go around with dynamite and blow up other people's property?"

Well, I went over there and interviewed folks and nobody denied it. They all admitted it freely. Then they said to me, "What are you going to do about it?" Well, I couldn't do anything. So I wrote to the man in New York and told him, "I am not going to do anything about it and the next time you want to come out here, you better not do anything about it either."

Colorado

———— ❧ ————

AFTER THE SHEEP HAD fed off the area close around Cedar City,
    they moved out into the other valley
        beyond Iron Springs and at first
            they grazed close around the water.
Then they moved up about four or five miles away
    up to what is known as Desert Mound.
They were trailing them back down to the water at Iron Springs
    whenever they needed to drink.
During one of the first winters they were in there,
    it come a heavy snow,
        probably a foot and a half to two feet of snow.
The herders who were handling the sheep,
    they sent word that the sheep were snowed in
        and they couldn't get them down
            to where they could get a drink
                and they were in bad shape.
So the call went out from the Bishop
    or whoever else was in charge of the co-op sheep
for all the men they could get,
    everybody to go out and tromp trails
        from Iron Springs up to Desert Mound
            so the sheep could walk down there
            and get a drink.

Well, of course, everybody that was able responded.
They come out and they worked all day tromping trails
    so they could get the sheep down to drink.
They were real disgusted and discouraged
     when they got them down there,
        and the sheep weren't interested in water—
            they'd had all the snow they wanted to.
That was quite a lesson they learned,
     one of the first lessons they learned,
        about handling sheep.

Utah

WHEN MY GRANDFATHER, Flay Lawrence,
     first bought the Hot Springs Ranch,
        above Glenns Ferry,
    he knew all the men up there.
For years, he'd run a grocery store in Glenns Ferry.
The first roundup started
     and Grandpa went out to join in.
The range boss told him to ride up King Hill Creek.
Now, King Hill Creek was the worst ride you could go on
     and Grandpa knew this.

So he rode on over and joined the rest of the group
     slated for King Hill Creek.
When he got there, one of the men got smart
     and called out, "Who are you, guy?"
"Why, I'm Mr. Horn."
"Huh?" and they all looked kinda bewildered. "Horn?"
"Yep. The first name is Green."
Grandpa had no problems getting accepted after that.

The next year, they asked him to ride King Hill Creek again.
"No," he said. "I've been up King Hill Creek.
    I'm not a greenhorn anymore."

Arizona

≈ Acknowledgements ≈

I HAVE INCURRED A number of debts in the process of gathering the stories for this book. As I visited libraries and archives around the West, I had the gracious assistance of many people. Among them are David Hoober, Arizona State Library; Jim Griffith, University of Arizona; Keith and Kathy Cunningham, Northern Arizona University; Hector Lee, Sonoma State University; Roland Dickison, Sacramento State University; Arthur Hansen and Gary Shumway, California State University, Fullerton; Julie Jones-Eddy, Colorado College; Richard Ellis, Fort Lewis State College; Zelda Rouillard, Western State College, Gunnison; Louie Attebery, College of Idaho; David Walter, Montana Historical Society; R. Thomas King, University of Nevada, Reno; Andrew Wiget, New Mexico State University; Sherry Sherman, University of Oregon; Barre Toelken, Barbara Walker, and Karen Krieger, Utah State University; and William A. Wilson, Brigham Young University.

Along the way I also enjoyed the hospitality and conversation of a number of friends and fellow folklorists, including Brian and Jennifer Attebery, Andrea Graham and Blanton Owen, Bert and Hannele Wilson, Keith and Kathy Cunningham, Meg Brady and Dave Stanley, John and Holly Dorst, and Jim and Loma Griffith. And members of my family—Mom and Dad in Las Cruces, New Mexico, Mary Pat and Harry in Craig, Colorado, John and Connie in Salem, Oregon, Ginny and John in Riverside, California, Joseph and Elizabeth in Chico, California, Maggie and Ken in Concord, California, and Patrick and Laura in San Francisco—also offered bed and board and welcome company as I traveled through their necks of the western woods. Many thanks to all for listening to me!

A portion of this research was supported by an NEH Travel to Collections grant in the summer of 1990.

Of course, the greatest debt is to the hundreds of people who told the stories and who allowed them to be recorded and archived for researchers like me to discover. I hope they are gratified to find that their words have reached a wider audience.

❦ A Note on the Texts ❧

I HAVE TAKEN CONSIDERABLE liberties with the texts as found in their archived forms. Some of the stories have been shortened; some have been reworded. None is a technically accurate transcription of the story as told or as represented in the archived text that I found. But I have not added anything to the stories that was not already there and, I hope, I have not eliminated anything essential to the story in the process of shaping it for presentation here.

The typographic presentation of the story texts was inspired by the technique of ethnopoetic transcription proposed by Dennis Tedlock in "Learning to Listen: Oral History as Poetry."[1] Following the spirit rather than the letter of Tedlock's model, I have tried to arrange the stories typographically in a way that leads the reader to understand their rhythms and sense as spoken, rather than written, texts. Some of the stories defied this treatment, and they are presented in standard sentence and paragraph form. But others, especially those that I heard or recorded myself, were easily adapted to the ethnopoetic format. I am aware that some readers may find the format distracting; I suggest that reading a few of the stories aloud should show how it is meant to work.

---

[1] Dennis Tedlock, "Learning to Listen: Oral History as Poetry," in *Envelopes of Sound: The Art of Oral History*, 2nd edition. Ed. Ronald J. Grele (Chicago: Precedent Publishing Co., 1985), pp. 106-125.

≋ Sources ≋

THE MATERIALS FOR this book were gathered from libraries and archives in eleven western states—Arizona, California, Colorado, Idaho, Montana, Nevada, New Mexico, Oregon, Utah, Washington, and Wyoming. In each state, at a minimum, I visited the state library or archives, the state historical society, and colleges or universities with substantial folklore and/or oral history collections. I also occasionally visited county and city public libraries with special collections, such as the Western History Collection at the Denver Public Library. Wherever I went, I looked for folklore, oral history, and local history collections. Sometimes I discovered narrative materials in unexpected places. In the Nevada State Historical Society, for instance, I discovered a collection of student history essays from the 1920s, products of a contest sponsored by the Woman's Clubs of Nevada, on such topics as "Stories Told by an Old-Timer." Another treasure trove was the Merrill Burlingame Collection at Montana State University, a collection of student papers written for Professor Burlingame's courses in Montana history from the 1940s through the 1970s.

The folklore archives at various western colleges and universities have proved to be a rich source of materials. I used the archives at the Southwest Folklore Center at the University of Arizona; the Arizona Friends of Folklore Collection at Northern Arizona University; the Archives of California and Western Folklore at UCLA; the Hector L. Lee Folklore Collections at Chico State University and Sonoma State University; the Folklore Archives at the University of California, Berkeley; the folklore collection at Sacramento State University; the Idaho Folklore Collection at the Idaho State Historical Society; the folklore collection at the Regional

Studies Center, College of Idaho; the Randall V. Mills Archives of Northwest Folklore at the University of Oregon; the Fife Folklore Collection at Utah State University; the University of Utah Folklore Collection; the Folklore Collection at Brigham Young University; and the student folklore collection in the American Studies Department at the University of Wyoming.

I also made use of a number of oral history collections. These included materials at Chico State University, California State University, Fullerton, Colorado State University, the Fort Collins Public Library, Colorado College, the Idaho State Historical Society, the Montana Historical Society, the University of Nevada, Reno, the University of New Mexico, New Mexico State University, Utah State University, Brigham Young University, and Washington State University.

The third major source of materials has been the folklore and local history collections of the WPA Federal Writers Project housed at the Arizona State Historical Society, the California State Library, the Colorado State Historical Society, the Idaho State Historical Society, Montana State University, the Nevada State Historical Society, the New Mexico State Archives, the Oregon State Library, the Utah State Historical Society, the Washington State Historical Society, and the Wyoming State Museum.

Sites Visited

Arizona
Northern Arizona University
Arizona State Library
Arizona Historical Society, Tucson
University of Arizona

California
University of California, Berkeley
Chico State University
California State University, Fullerton
University of California, Los Angeles
Sonoma State University
California State Library
Sacramento State University

Colorado
University of Colorado
Colorado College

Colorado Historical Society
Denver Public Library
University of Denver
Fort Lewis State College
Colorado State University
Fort Collins Public Library
Mesa County Public Library
Museum of Western Colorado
Routt County Public Library

Idaho

Idaho State Historical Society
College of Idaho

Montana

Montana State University
Montana Historical Society

Nevada

University of Nevada, Reno
Nevada State Historical Society

New Mexico

University of New Mexico
New Mexico State University

Oregon

University of Oregon
Oregon Historical Society

Utah

Southern Utah State College
Utah State University
Brigham Young University
Utah State Historical Society
University of Utah

Washington

Washington State University
University of Washington
Washington State Historical Society
Vancouver Public Library

Wyoming

Wyoming State Museum
University of Wyoming
Rock Springs Public Library

Born in California, Barbara Allen Bogart studied literature and history at the University of Southern California, then earned an M.A. in literature from San Francisco State University, and M.A. and Ph.D. degrees in folklore from UCLA. Recently, she served as the historian at the Wyoming State Museum and taught courses for the University of Wyoming. Before moving to Wyoming in 1991, she was a member of the American Studies faculty at the University of Notre Dame for ten years.

Dr. Bogart has twenty years' experience in oral history and folklore fieldwork, concentrating her research activities in the western states. She is the author or editor of three books, *A Sense of Place: American Regional Cultures* (1990), *Homesteading the High Desert* (1987), and *From Memory to History: Using Oral Sources in Local History Research* (1981). She has also published more than two dozen articles and essays on oral history, western history, and regional culture for professional journals.

She and her husband, Dan, live in Evanston, Wyoming.

Mary Patricia Ettinger is the illustrator of both the cover and the interior pages. She has been drawing and painting since childhood. She currently specializes in landscapes and works primarily with colored pencils and acrylics, using the watercolor method.

Her work has appeared in shows in California and in Colorado. She resides in Craig, Colorado.

The text is composed in
eleven-point Adobe Palatino.
Display type is SMC Cheyenne.
This book is printed on
sixty-pound Glatfelter Supple Opaque
acid-free, recycled paper
by Thomson-Shore.